COX'S
FRAGMENTA II

FURTHER FOLIOS
FROM HISTORY

EDITED BY SIMON MURPHY

© British Library Board. All Rights Reserved 937.g.1–94.
All illustrations courtesy of Lillian Low.

First published 2012

The History Press
The Mill, Brimscombe Port
Stroud, Gloucestershire, GL5 2QG
www.thehistorypress.co.uk

© Simon Murphy for selection and editorial matter, 2012

British Library Cataloguing in Publication Data.
A catalogue record for this book is available from the British Library.

ISBN 978 0 7524 6507 4

Typesetting and origination by The History Press
Printed in India
Manufacturing managed by Jellyfish Print Solutions Ltd

~

INTRODUCTION

Unsurprisingly, the content of Cox's bewildering collection remained consistently inconsistent as its curator moved from 1822 (his seventieth year) to 1834. His sources – predominantly the newspapers of London and Birmingham – continued to feed the popular appetite for local, national and international news; the mixture is spiced with sport, rumour, fashion, gossip, satire and vituperation. What is unexpected is the mushrooming of content collected each year. While the first half of the ninety-four volumes covered a period of thirty years, the second part spans only ten. Why such an increase in the average?

The history of the press at the time offers no clues; there had certainly been no sudden drop in the price of a newspaper. Until 1836 the stamp duty on a paper stood at 4*d*, and furthermore King George's six acts of 1819 had required all publishers and printers (of periodicals that cost less than 6*d* and were published one or more times a month) to post a bond to ensure their 'good behaviour'.

While newspaper consumption outside Britain was largely on the increase, these financial constraints on printers and publishers kept both prices high and readership relatively elite. Mr E.L. Bulwer, writer and MP for Lincoln 1832–41, declared in the House of Commons that the duty was a 'tax on knowledge' and that periodicals were a luxury.[1] On 14 June 1832, the day of Bulwer's speech, a copy of *The Times* cost 7*d* – around the same time a plate of meat and pint of ale could be had for 9*d*.[2]

Knowing as little as we do about Cox himself, it would be guesswork to suggest personal reasons for his increased interest in obtaining copies of the day's news (though one could reasonably imagine advancing years gave him a little more time to read). What can be gleaned from the *Fragmenta* is a growing concern for accuracy and order in his collection. In the earlier volumes of his scrapbook, articles were pasted roughly chronologically, but with no concern for pairing the piece with its date, or source publication; however, in later volumes

---

1 As reported in *The Hull Packet and Humber Mercury*, Tuesday 26 June 1832. His motion to repeal the duty was finally successful in 1855. He had more rapid success with an 1833 bill that established dramatic copyright.

2 *The Caledonian Mercury*, Saturday 19 December 1835.

articles are purposefully cut out to keep title and date. Often a column of text is pasted in its entirety. Sometimes whole papers are neatly folded and included. This decision to bracket articles with their particulars necessarily means more material is saved and the collection fills out.

What is also evident is that this concern for order leads Cox to interact with his materials in a slightly more critical way. On a few occasions he adds the date, publication title or even specific section of the paper by hand,[3] and very rarely he even pens marginalia relating to the content. In the bottom gutter of the front page of *The Times* from Monday 14 March 1831 (v.87, p.60) we are greeted with the following in a clear hand: 'Number Immense! 153 adverts! the whole amount to about eight hundred.'[4] Not only did Cox collect and store the papers of his day voraciously, but he was also reading them with an eye for content and proportion.

Are we surprised that Cox chose to write down such thoughts? Whether or not the collection itself was kept private or opened to friends by Cox, we

---

3   He adds the section title and date: 'Parliamentary Foreign Affairs. May. 1. 1823' (v.57, p.164).

4   That Cox found the opportunity to count them suggests he may indeed have been richer in free time.

know it was his intention to leave the volumes that comprised his life's work to the British Museum. He would have been increasingly conscious that at some point the trove would be examined, and so his pen's rare incursions on to the pages of the *Fragmenta* must be seen as an aware form of self-display. The reference to the number of adverts, which goes beyond simply recording the figure, expresses a little overplayed astonishment and helps construct a ghost of his character within the collection. In most places the papers exist undisturbed, but in others the pen creeps in, reminding us whose guest we are. This quiet entrance raises a question: what kind of reader did Cox seek to be seen as?

The material selected is the first indication of Cox's interests; but those pages that have been annotated are proof of a more active curiosity. Auction catalogues are included, the sum each object made often neatly filled in. Not only did he, or someone he knew, attend sales of furniture, coins, prints, books, paintings and so on, but what's more, it seems, they stayed for the entire event and saw each object sold. Poems also appear, copied out or pasted among the cuttings, with one short verse titled 'Upon the Death of Lord Nelson' written by Cox himself. Within the *Fragmenta* there are also papers and notes, pasted complete with the names (in Cox's hand) of the prominent individuals that presented him with the ephemera. The list includes Rear Admiral Sir Charles Cunningham, Matthias Attwood MP and a 'Chandos' who writes from Pall Mall (the Duke himself?).[5] The collection also gains a cosmopolitan edge from the geographical range of the publications Cox obtained. Among others there are editions of *Le Constitutionnel* (France), *The Conception-Bay Mercury* (Canada) and *The Canton Register* (China).[6]

It's easy to understand that like many men of his time Cox read the papers to stay abreast of events, but he is unusual in his desire to keep them. While others consigned their old papers to package wrapping or kindling, what compelled Cox to cut his up after reading and paste them into volumes? Why include other printed matter such as catalogues and speeches, before donating the results to the most impressive bibliographic institute he could?

The period in which Cox lived witnessed a huge number of fundamental transformations, changes George Eliot (writing of 1832) described as 'the present quickening in the general pace of things'.[7] The country

5   v.18, p.158; v.86, p.14; and v.85, p.122.

6   v.87, p.50; v.87, p.102; and v.90, p.74.

7   Eliot, George, *Middlemarch*, chapter 65.

moved from a collection of mainly rural settlements to expanding cities driven by steam and commerce; the government had begun combating epidemic disease with organised inoculation programmes; the new Metropolitan Police force was in action; parliamentary reform took place and the Far East and South America were opening up as potentially huge sources of trade and revenue. With change so ubiquitous, the daily paper must have been eagerly anticipated. These publications now offer a tremendous perspective on these past events – something Cox, with his collection destined for the sanctity of the British Museum, clearly anticipated. And he wasn't alone. On Thursday 26 March 1801 an auction was held on the Strand. The advertisement read:

> In this day's sale will also be offered to the public an extraordinary COLLECTION of NEWSPAPERS, consisting of upwards of three hundred Volumes, perfect and half bound, from which the Literati may select Materials for forming a complete history of literature, and of the Times in which the newspapers were written.[8]

8 *The Morning Post and Gazetteer*, Tuesday 24 March 1801.

The literati, however, have not flocked to Cox's *Fragmenta*. Indeed, apart from C.B. Oldman's 1966 commentary on the work, it has never been – as far as we know – used by or useful to a soul. This can largely be put down to the difficulty of navigating the vast collection. To discover the newsworthy events of a particular day one would have to pluck a volume from the ninety-four almost at random, find the dates it encompasses and repeat the process, refining until the desired date was discovered. Even at the end of this long business you would have at best the one or two papers Cox pasted for the day. (He might not even have bought one.) Far easier to use an indexed online database of scanned papers.

Between 1804 and 1838 a number of tiny electromagnetic signals were sent, the first signs of changes that would eventually affect the world just as significantly as steam power. Inventors, such as Sömmering, Salvá i Campillo, Morse, Fothergill, Weber and Gauss were investigating the potential of electric telegraphy, a process by which messages could be sent instantaneously and over great distances. Pronounced in 1837 as 'one of the most important and extraordinary discoveries of this inventive age',[9] initial applications included the improvement of signalling on railway lines and the reporting of crime. Relatively recent improvements in technology have helped the concept behind those first experiments to blossom; e-mail and the internet allow communication and information transfer to increase dramatically. The consequence of this new ability seems to be a definition of information coloured by the potential and advantages of modern technology; information is assumed to be immediate, transparent and searchable, organised and navigated at the click of a mouse.

But imagine divesting yourself of laptop, broadband, e-mail and mobile. It is 1820. The gas lighting on your street has only just been installed. Each night before bed you wind your pocket watch, setting the time as best you can against the church bells of London which ring, the hours staggered and unpunctual, as evening falls. It's a world away from search engines and social networking – modern essentials we have learned to synchronise our thinking with. Indeed we are now such effective users of information technology that it often takes us only a few seconds to discover the information we require.

---

9   *The Morning Chronicle*, Saturday 30 December 1837.

Cox's collection is the antithesis: it cannot be searched, repackaged, simplified or stored; but this does not render it obsolete. Rather it enforces the serendipity of browsing and renders the opportunity to pursue a tangent ever present. Every cutting included in these two volumes has been stumbled upon and perhaps there is even something in this anachronistic approach that brings us a little closer to the period that intrigues: despite the order that technology has allowed us to impose on the past we sit down to the papers to read history unfolding precisely as Cox would have – open to surprise.

~

DRURY-LANE THEATRE

Mr. Macready last night sustained the character of
Macbeth. His performance, though occasionally
irradiated by flashes of genius, was, on the whole,
entitled to little more than the praise of being coldly
correct. Mr. Wallack's *Macduff* was energetic without
rant. The choruses were given in an excellent style.
When the tragedy is next performed, it is humbly
requested that a smaller quantity of sulphur may
be used in illuminating the shadowy descents of
Banquo. Last night Mr. Macready was for some
minutes enveloped in a dense cloud of sulphurous
smoke, which eventually concealed him from view.
The cloud soon made its way amongst the audience,
who were simultaneously seized with a fit of
coughing, which lasted for a quarter of an hour.

The Times, Friday 31 October 1823 (v.60, p.57)

The following anecdote, as told by the captain of a
whale ship which was at Valparaiso, shows of what

unshakable fortitude the hard sons of Neptune are possessed, and what indifference they evince even under the severest misfortunes. 'One morning,' says he 'as we were cruising about in search of whales, we espied an especially fine looking one, and at no great distance from us. We immediately manned 4 boats, and soon came up to this monster of the deep, which proved to be a whale of the sperm kind. We attacked him, and in return for a death-wound which we inflicted, he, as is frequently the case with these ferocious animals, stove in one of the boats. In the confusion which ensued, one poor fellow unluckily came within reach of the whale, who, although in the agonies of death, made shift to draw one of his legs into his mouth. The thigh was pierced with one of his tusks, and consequently broken. Luckily for the sailor, however, the whale began to gasp, which afforded him an opportunity to escape from the jaws of immediate death. On being carried to the ship, it was found necessary to amputate the leg above the joint, which operation was borne with the greatest equanimity. Shortly after (continued the captain,) I asked him what were his feelings when he was in the whale's mouth. "Why," says he, "I thought he might furnish 60 barrels of pretty good oil!"'

The Times, **Tuesday 10 February 1824 (v.62, p.1)**

∾

VACCINATION

It appears from the reports of the National Vaccine Board to the Right Hon. Robert Peel, that the applications for lymph have been much more than usually numerous – a proof that the confidence of the world in vaccination is increasing, particularly since the Parliamentary establishment, where the inoculating matter is always to be procured. Since the last report, lymph had been despatched to the East and West Indies, to Ceylon, to the Cape of Good Hope, the island of Mauritius, the coast of Africa, New South Wales, and to France and Italy, &c. The report then states that it has been distributed in this kingdom with great success, 'for the small pox has prevailed as an epidemic with more than ordinary malignity in various parts of this island lately, and has committed great ravages in those districts where it found victims unprotected against it by a previous process.' The total number vaccinated from 1818 to 1822 in the United Kingdom (excepting the capital) is 327,521, and the total by the stationary vaccinators for the same time 34,275. In 1821 there were 90,000 persons vaccinated in Ceylon; 20,149 in the Presidency of Fort William; and 22,478 in that of Bombay.

The Times, Tuesday 10 February 1824 (v.62, p.4)

The benign yet powerful properties of that most esteemed cosmetic Rowland's Kalydor stands pre-eminent; it thoroughly exterminates eruption, tan, pimples, freckles, redness, and all cutaneous imperfection whatsoever; arrays the neck, hands, and arms in matchless whiteness; bestows on the complexion a juvenile bloom; renovates beauty when on the decline; realises it where before absent, and sustains it in pristine splendour to the latest period of life. To mothers nursing their offspring it is essentially serviceable in healing soreness, and reducing inflammation, so frequently following this otherwise pleasing pursuit of maternal affection. To gentlemen, Rowlands Kalydor will be found an infallible specific in allaying the smarting irritability of the face, and will render shaving, heretofore a painful, now a pleasurable operation.

Various, *c.* June 1825 (v.70, p.5)

~

WOLVES IN RUSSIA

The following is the official account of the devastations committed by the wolves in the Government of Livonia only, in the year 1823: they devoured – horses, 1,841; foals, 1,243; horned cattle, 1,807; calves, 733; sheep, 15,182; lambs, 726; goats, 2,545; kids, 183; swine, 4,190; sucking pigs, 312; dogs, 703; geese, 673.

The Times, **Tuesday 7 June 1825 (v.70, p.20)**

~

EXTRAORDINARY INTRUSION

On Sunday last, four ladies from Newcastle-upon-Tyne applied at the coach office in Liverpool for four seats in the coach from the Woodside ferry to Chester. They were told that the whole of the inside was vacant, being six seats; and in order to prevent intrusion, they engaged all of the inside places.

Having crossed the Mersey in the steam-boat, they boarded the coach, and proceeded on their way to Chester, giving particular direction at the Ferry-house that 'They must not be intruded upon by any person!' Their request, it would seem, was not complied with to the letter, inasmuch as on the arrival of the coach near Eastham, the passengers *on deck* were alarmed by loud shrieks from the cabin passengers. The pilot slackened sail, laid the helm a larboard, and drew up; but the astonishment of the coachman may be more easily conceived than described, when he discovered one of the ladies in the embraces – not of some sly rogue who had imperceptibly climbed in at the window, but – of a huge, black bear! All hands were piped, and the belward was called for, when with some difficulty Bruin was detached from his grip, and the lady escaped with no other loss than that of her shawl, which was torn, and the suffering of extreme fright, which naturally ensued. It may be necessary to explain how Bruin got into such excellent company. It appeared his keeper was conducting him from Lancashire into Chester to a bear's college, of which there are several in the latter county, in order to teach him to dance and obtain the other accomplishments so necessary to the education of a

polished bear. Being rather young, and probably of a delicate habit of body, Bruin's master contracted with the coachman for a berth in the boot, and into it was the poor animal put. But not relishing so confined a space he fortunately found out a hole in the panelling at the back of the coach, and by dint of scratching and biting (which were not heard owing to the noise of the wheels) the bear found means to insinuate his elegant form amongst the ladies, and round the neck of one was he found in the way described. It is scarcely necessary to say, that for this very unmannered intrusion, Bruin was expelled from the vehicle, and such a consequence should operate as a warning on all presumptuous bears.

The Times, **Thursday 9 June 1825 (v.70, p.34)**

~

ACCIDENT AT THE

SURREY THEATRE

On Monday evening, during the first act of *Jocko*, a serious accident before Mons. Simon, who plays the ourang-outang. He was leaping from one branch of a tree to another, when he accidentally fell, and is supposed broke his leg. M. Simon was conveyed home in a senseless state.

[NOTE: The drama of *Jocko, or The Monkey from Brazil* was based on a novel by Charles de Paugens and was variously reworked during the 1820s, appearing as a two-act 'Melo-Drama' as well as ballet. There was at the time a particular vogue for actors aping animals, and so popular was Jocko that audiences demanded that the original ending (in which Jocko, after saving both the son and fortune, is shot and dies in a burst of 'tam-tams') was re-written to ensure the heroic simian survived.

The Morning Post also made mention of the misfortune suffered by M. Simon 'who, since the introduction of the piece, so finely performed the arduous part of the Brazilian Ourang-Outang. In the first act, in making one of his terrific leaps, he came with such violence to ground as to make a fracture on the ancle'. (*The Morning Post*, Wednesday 15 June 1825)]

The Times, Wednesday 15 June 1825 (v.70, p.47)

King Lear – The representative of *Gloucester*, in this tragedy, lately in a provincial town, was taken ill at a short notice, and another gentleman was found who was 'rough studied' in the character. He got on famously until the scene where he has his eyes put out, and then he was obliged to beg permission to 'read the rest of the part'.

The Times, **Friday 8 July 1825 (v.70, p.130)**

At the Mansion House on Saturday a charge was preferred against an individual for adulterating flour, which led to a conversion and disclosure of great interest to the public. It appears from the testimony of Mr. Clarke of the Apothecaries' Company that the iniquitous practice of adulterating flour is carried on to a most fearful extent. At Hull no less than 1,457 sacks of a composition called flour had been prepared for exportation, which, on being analysed, proved to be one-third composed of ground bones and plaster of Paris; the property was ordered to be destroyed, and the owner or owners ordered to pay a fine of £10,000. The same gentleman also made a singular statement with respect to tea; he had lately analysed some Souchong tea, and found that there was 25 per cent. of *lead ore* in it.

The Morning Post, Tuesday 26 July 1825
(v.71, p.22)

❖

On Saturday night, the people in a grocer's shop in Campbell-street, were much alarmed by a young woman who, while standing at the counter, suddenly uttered a piercing scream, pressed her hand firmly upon her bosom, and rushed wildly out of the shop. The girl instantly ran to her own house, where the cause of the mysterious conduct was discovered – a *large rat* was found – we almost blush to say – nearly crushed to death by the bones of her corset!

The Times, Wednesday 10 August 1825 (v.71, p.93)

~

GIGANTIC ORGANIC REMAINS

We lately mentioned that the bones of a non-descript animal of immense size, and larger than any bones that have hitherto been noticed by naturalists, have been discovered 20 miles from New Orleans, in the alluvial ground formed by the Mississippi river, and the lakes, but a short distance from the sea. A fragment of the cranium is stated to measure 22 feet in length; in its broadest part four feet high, and perhaps nine inches thick. The New Orleans people are much puzzled, as well they might be, to ascertain the class of animals to which these extraordinary bones belong. From the circumstance of ambergris being found on the interior surface of the largest bone, it is supposed that they are of marine origin; and the editor of the *New Orleans Gazette*, who examined them, says that this examination has convinced him of the truth of the extraordinary relations given by Kircher of the Kraken and Norway sea-snake; and, judging from the portion of the cranium which he had seen, he concludes, that if this monster was of the balanæ species, its length could not be less than 250 feet.

The Times, **Wednesday 10 August 1825**
(v.71, p.95)

≈

WARWICK SUMMER ASSIZES

The following is an abstract of the offences and sentences of the prisoners: –
IMPRISONMENT.
Richard Ford, for stealing a watch, in this town; Samuel Bannister, for assaulting with the intent to rob, in this town – *two years*. – William Twist, for stealing fourteen pistols, in this town – *eighteen months*. – William Kempson, for stealing a bible, &c. in this town; Bennet Barton, for stealing a watch, in this town; Thomas Bayley, for stealing a till containing silver, at Henley-in-Arden; Ann Nokes, for stealing wearing apparel, at Sherborne; Sarah Burbridge, for stealing linen, at Great Pockington – *one year*. – Thos. Harrington, for stealing a watch, in this town; William Stevens, for stealing mixed metal,

in this town; John Fitzpatrick, for stealing shoes, in this town; Henry Humphries, for stealing needles, at Ipsley; John Luccock, for stealing six rabbits, at Aston – *six months* – Edwin Taylor, for stealing three guns, in this town; Henrey Web, for stealing sacks, at Milverton; Thomas Homer, for stealing one gown, at Aston – *three months*. – William Yandall and Thomas Holloway, for stealing a smock-frock, &c. at Edgebaston; William George, for stealing a saw, at Aston; George Bonham, for stealing bacon, at Leamington – *two months*. – John Whitehouse, for stealing a hat, at Aston – *one month*.

The Times, Thursday 11 August 1825 (v.71, p.97)

~

ANTHONY PIG

This was a common nickname for a dangler among our older writers: its origin, which is rather curious, was as follows: – Philip of France, son of Louis the Fat, was killed, riding one day in the streets of Paris, by a pig's running between his horses legs and throwing him down. In consequence of this accident, an order was made that pigs should not, on pain of the severest penalties, run about the public street; but an exception was made in favour of those which belonged to the Monks of the Convent of St. Anthony; out of the partiality in which King Louis held that Saint. Whence the term 'Anthony Pig' (according to several French writers) applied to any idler who seemed to run up and down as he pleased. Goldsmith, in his *She Stoops to Conquer*, makes Tony Lumpkin tell his cousin 'not to be following him around like a Tantony Pig.'

The Times, Monday 22 August 1825 (v.71, p.182)

A melancholy accident happened at Bracklay Distillery, near Nairn, on Saturday last. John MacDonald, one of the men employed in the distillery, while stretching himself, after getting up in the morning, overbalanced himself, and fell into the mash tun; he was speedily taken out by a person with whom he had been talking when he fell, but was so dreadfully scalded that he only survived until the next day, in great torture. The deceased was a man of sober habits.

The Times, Monday 22 August 1825 (v.71, p.188)

One of the mountaineers of Auvergne, whose trade it is to exhibit live monkeys and dancing bears, had also trained half a dozen dogs to different exercises. One mounted guard, with a gun and a little sabre; another made perilous leaps; a third jumped like a frog; a fourth, clad in a black robe, and placed in a chair, maintained a thesis, by howling incessantly at the others, who replied in return by barking at him. In short, this little corps of four-footed comedians formed the revenue of the master; for mankind pays better for what amuses them, than for lessons in wisdom and prudence. Through a jealousy too common among people of that same trade, a dealer in bears poisoned five of the *dramatis personae* of his rival, who, affected at so serious a loss (for five dancers cannot be made in a day) fell sick and took to his bed.

Caledonian Mercury, Monday 12 September 1825
(v.71, p.225)

~

PREPARATION OF

COFFEE AT ROSETTA

One of the most curious sights in Rosetta, so famous for the finest Mocha coffee, is the preparation of that article for use. After roasting the coffee, it is pounded in immense mortars; three Arabs working at a time with immense pestles, each as large as a man can raise. The capacity of the bottom of the mortar being only equal to the reception of one of these at a time, the pestles are raised according to the measure of an air sung by an attendant Arab, who sits near the mortar. The main purport of this curious accompaniment is to prevent the hand and arms of a boy kneeling near the mortar being crushed to atoms. The boy's arm is always within the mortar, which allows room for the pestle to pass in turn without bruising him, if he places it in time against the side of the vessel; but, as after every stroke he must stir up the powder at the bottom of the vessel with his fingers, if the precise period of each blow were not marked by the measure of the song, his arm would be struck off. A sight of this process is sufficient to explain the cause of this very impalpable nature of the coffee used in Turkey, where the infusion more resembles the appearance of chocolate than of coffee, as we prepare them in England.

[NOTE: the relationship between the British and their coffee has come rather a long way since the 1674 *Women's Petition Against Coffee*, which blamed coffee houses for the 'very sensible Decay of that Old English Vigour ... [by promoting] the excessive use of that Newfangled, Abominable, Heathenish liquor called Coffee, which ... has so Eunucht our Husbands and Crippled our more kind gallants they come from it with nothing moist but their snotty noses, nothing stiffe but their Joints'. This was not enough to halt the popularity of coffee, and during a botanical lecture on berries in 1823, Dr Thornton gave a very different opinion of its powers, suggesting it as a cure for scorbutic humours, putrid fever and attacks of asthma. 'A cup of coffee,' he explains, 'strengthens and exhilarates our mental and bodily faculties; and nothing can be more refreshing either to the studious or the laborious than a dish of good coffee.'

(*The Morning Post*, Thursday 14 August 1823). Healthy or not, the London Watch also wanted coffee houses shut (but for very different reasons to the women of 1674). They claimed: 'it hath become a practise of late to open shops or rooms for the sale of ready-made coffee, tea, or other liquors, and to keep such shops or rooms open during the whole or the greater part of the night, thereby affording shelter and accommodation to thieves, prostitutes, and disorderly persons, and tending greatly to the encouragement of robberies, and to the concealment of stolen property.' (*The Standard*, Monday 10 December 1827)]

The Times, Tuesday 4 October 1825 (v.72, p.199)

The present Rajah of Mysore's elephant carriage is probably the most magnificent conveyance ever seen. Its interior is a double sofa for six persons, covered with dark green velvet and gold, surmounted by an awning of cloth of gold, in the shape of two scalloped domes, meeting over the centre, and surrounded by a richly ornamental veranda, supported by light, elegant fluted gilt pillars; the whole is capable of containing sixty persons, and is about twenty-two feet in height. It moves on four wheels, the hinder ones eight feet in diameter, with a breadth of twelve feet between them. It is drawn by six immense elephants, with a driver on each, harnessed to the carriages by traces, as in England, and their huge heads covered with a sort of cap, made of richly embroidered cloth. The pace at which they move is a sort of slow trot, of about seven miles an hour; they are very steady, and the springs of the carriage particularly easy. As it is crane-necked, the elephants turn round with it with the greatest facility.

The Times, **Thursday 7 October 1825 (v.73, p.81)**

FONTHILL ABBEY

(We have received the following communication this morning. The name of the writer, and his residence, are added. We lay it before our readers without being able to confirm or contradict the statement.)

TO THE EDITOR

Sir,– The Post having gone out, I embrace this opportunity of giving you the earliest intelligence of the fall of that fine (but flimsy) architectural structure, Fonthill Abbey. The tower fell in at three o'clock this afternoon, destroying the hall, the whole of the octagon, and a great part of the galleries, north and south, together with the first crimson room, having descended into the fountain court, leaving the grand entrance standing with the organ in *statu que*, and the statue of the late Alderman Beckford in its niche, as if it remained to point out the ruins of his son's ambition.

I am just returned from the Abbey, and am happy to say that only one accident has occurred, although the servants were engaged in taking out some of the windows and had fortunately just escaped in time to avoid being buried in the ruins.

Mr. Farquhar has taken the precaution to move to the East Wing, together with Mrs. Mortimer and her children. The latter had been in the daily habit of playing in the gardens.

The only surprise is, on beholding the slightness of the foundation walls, that it has so long stood the violent gales that it has been exposed to.

I remain Sir, your humble servant, J.F. Fonthill, Gifford, Wilts, Dec 21.

The Times, Saturday 24 December 1825 (v.74, p.216)

On Wednesday afternoon, the inhabitants of Fonthill Abbey were alarmed by a most tremendous crash, which seemed like nothing more nor less than the sudden crushing into ruins of the whole building. Their terror was, however, soon abated by finding that the lofty tower had fallen, and burst through that part of the building that nearly adjoined it, without occasioning any personal injury whatever. It appears that the proprietor (Mr. Farquhar) had strong apprehensions of this lamentable occurrence, and had removed most of the costly embellishments, to secure them from the impending danger. The cause of this event is not attributable to any fault of the architect, but to the instability of the materials. It not being at first designed to be raised to any thing near its height, the architect had of course fixed the foundation proportionately; and when it was proposed to raise it to its remarkable elevation, the building was far too advanced to allow any adoption to render the foundation sufficiently strong to support it; and in order to meet the wishes of the then proprietor (Wm. Beckford Esq.) in raising it to its noble and commanding height, and thereby add so greatly to the magnificence of the whole, the architect was obliged to use wood in its erection. But, alas! this was not of that quality to render so beautiful a structure a lasting monument of the taste of the designer, and, as a display of architectural elegance, an honour to the county.

(From *The Bath Journal*)
***The Times*, Saturday 24 December 1825 (v.74, p.241)**

❖

Mr. Beckford, the late owner of Fonthill, has directed his bier, upon which his coffin is to be carried, to be manufactured of elegant workmanship, by an upholsterer at Bath, and to be placed in his private apartment as a *memento mori*. It is affirmed that the tower which he has built upon Lansdown-hill is the burial-place where it will be ultimately deposited.

[NOTE: William Beckford, author of the gothic novel *Vathek*, was variously a spendthrift, MP, art collector and patron;

he is, however, perhaps best remembered for his buildings, which were architectural translations of personal characteristics and an endeavour at recreating something of the sublime. The building of Fonthill Abbey began in 1796, and the result – a colossal mixture of architectural styles and materials – was fit for habitation in 1812. Twice the 90m-high central tower fell in, but Beckford continued to live there with no one but his servants. Distaining society, Beckford surrounded himself with the most opulent paintings, porcelain, mirrors, books, coffers and chandeliers. When the outside world (in the shape of horsemen and hounds from a local hunt) infringed upon his private monument, Beckford had a 12ft-high wall built around his land – an 8-mile undertaking. The central tower's weakness was its fabric; to speed construction, timber with a coating of cement was used, and though this lasted long enough for Beckford to sell his masterpiece to John Farquhar, it did finally fall in 1825. It had been Beckford's initial whim that, after his death, he was to be interred in the tower of Fonthill itself, with his naked body exposed to the elements (but protected from birds by a grating). As the building survived for only a third of Beckford's life, this was impossible.]

The Morning Chronicle, **Saturday 1 November 1828 (v.80, p.60)**

London Literary and Publishing Society,
No. 23, Old Bond Street

THE very high prices of new Books, whether original works or reprints, have long been a subject of just complaint with the public; and at a period like the present, which is characterised by ardour for information, is felt with particular severity: under these circumstances this establishment has been formed, with the auspices of several literary and patriotic men, for the purpose of remedying an evil, calculated in so great a degree, to prevent the diffusion of knowledge and the moral improvement of society; it engages itself to supply the public with new books, such as shall recommend themselves by their correctness and style, both to the scholar and to the man of taste, at a reduction, on the average, of nearly one half of the present prices.

The means by which this Society will chiefly effect this important national object, which also constitutes its main and distinguishing feature, is this, the *publications will be produced for, and offered to the public, directly, and at the first price, instead of through the medium of booksellers.* On the system of publishing which has hitherto prevailed, new books do not reach the public until they have passed through several hands, and have had from 40 to

50 per cent. added to the first price; by the plan of offering its works to the public, in the first instance, this large addition will at once be saved to the book buyer; this, with the further means of reduction, afforded by the extensive scale of their contract in paper and printing, and by disposing of their works in ready money, will enable the Society amply to fulfil its important engagements.

Mr. Septimus Prowett has the entire management of the publishing department.

[NOTE: In 1826 the British book trade suffered a major crash, partly a hangover of the generally poor financial health of the country in the preceding years and also partly due to the unimpressive quality of literary output at the time. The little-known publisher Septimus Prowett wrangled with a variety of material in his search for commercial success. Although the 260-page text *The Art of Preserving the Hair on Philosophical Principles* never managed a second edition, he deserves plaudits for contracting the artist John Martin to engrave twenty-four plates to illustrate his 1827 edition of Milton's *Paradise Lost*. The work appeared in Imperial Quarto edition, and, according to the publisher, would impress due to the artist's 'peculiar adaptations of his powers to the lofty undertaking of embodying the stupendous and preternatural imagery of the Paradise Lost' (*The Morning Post*, Thursday 18 January 1827). In this assumption he was perhaps correct. The epic images of Martin were to inspire a generation of Romantics, with the Brontës choosing his work for a wall at Haworth.]

Birmingham Journal and General Advertiser, Monday 2 January 1826 (v.74, p.275)

If every house now in a state of insolvency were to be allowed to utter bills payable in three years upon the amount of its supposed assets, and the partners were then to be put in possession of those assets, and to carry on business as they could, what would be the result, but that a fresh commercial crash must take place at the end of the three years? The country would never be out of embarrassments.

The Times, **Tuesday 21 February 1821 (v.76, p.1)**

We cannot help reverting to the mischiefs and even cruelties likely to ensue from the excessive issue of small paper by the Bank. Country banks are now calling in their one and two pound notes; time and use are also wearing them away; and no fresh stamps are allowed. The small notes of the Bank will begin, therefore, to protrude themselves into all the provinces as the exclusive medium of barter among the manufacturing classes. And how are they to be guarded from imitation; or how, being imitated, are the forged notes to be detected? Forgeries were most afflictingly frequent when the one and the two pound notes of the Bank made up but a trifling part of the small note currency of the realm, and when they were only circulated among the more knowing Chapmen of London, who had the means of detection. What will be the case when they pass into remote districts, and constitute the whole paper-currency of the laborious classes, who may travel miles before they can find a person competent and willing to say whether a note is real or forged?

The Times, Tuesday 21 February 1826 (v.76, p.1)

❖

A young woman, who had been particularly fortunate in Exeter Market laſt week, in the diſpoſal of her turkeys and other Chriſtmas commodities, was observed by some sharper to have plenty of change, and accordingly he bargained for 2*s.* worth of eggs and presented a bill, asking for change for £5. Four pounds 8*s.* were returned, and it was the next day before it was discovered to be a note for *five pence*, payable at the 'Bank of Elegance.'

[NOTE: Between 1797 and 1825 the country's first one and two pound notes were printed, and due to their higher circulation they quickly became the obvious targets for forgers. In the year 1820 alone, over 29,000 forged notes were known to be presented, with a total value of over £33,000. As the banknote crisis spread, and more felons were convicted of forging small sums, the punishment for forgery was mitigated from death to transportation.]

Birmingham Journal and General Advertiser, Saturday 3 January 1829 (v.81, p.81)

To the Editor of the Times

Sir

Last week a number of principle merchants in the city waited on my Lord Liverpool, requesting a loan on their stock in hand for which they could not get a ready sale. On being told Minsters could not relieve them in the way they wished, they urged something be done, or there would be a national bankruptcy; they could not go on without the loan on goods was effected, and his lordship finally referred them to the Bank.

Now Sir I wish to trouble these said respectable merchants &c. with a word or two on this subject.

The facility with which you, the merchants and traders of this country, have been able to create a capital, by getting cash for your paper, has caused the excessive speculation, the effect of which is the present distress, in which you have deemed it expedient to urge the first Minister of this country to become your pawnbroker. Truly respectable this!

Formerly the persons who filled the situations you now do were content if they could keep a good house over their heads in the situation best suited to the business they carried on, and were always there to be found, except for a holyday or two in the summer. Now, there is not one of you who has less than two houses, and many of you five – your very clerks have their country villas, which have sprung up like mushrooms round town – with all the etceteras of carriages, horses, butlers, cooks, footmen, grooms, and ladies-maids. Your present style of living has fully kept pace with your other extravagancies.

Instead of bending your ways to Whitehall to impress upon the Minister your sense of his negligence in not legislating to obviate your self-sought difficulties, begin to legislate at home – reform your firesides, curtail your expenses, give up four of your horses, or, in other words, keep but one, and look strictly after your business; for, believe me, in five-and-twenty years more, if your extravagancies keep pace with those of the last five-and-twenty, the profit on the trade of the whole world will not support the traders of the city of London.

THE UNFEE'D ADVISER

The Times, **Monday 6 March 1826 (v.76, p.51)**

~

LONDON GYMNASTIC SOCIETY

A number of persons met yesterday evening, pursuant to notice, at the theatre of the Mechanics' Institute, in Southampton-buildings, Chancery-lane, to consider the expediency of establishing a school for the teaching and practise of active bodily exercise in the metropolis.

Dr. Gilchrist then took the chair, and proceeded to explain the general advantage of what was proposed to his hearers; in which, if we do not go quite so far as to believe, with the worthy Doctor, that dancing masters are the longest lived (as well as legged) class of subjects in His Majesty's dominions, or that he (Dr. Gilchrist) by the practise of gymnastics in his youth might have extended himself to a height of six feet, from a stature of about five feet four, we are nevertheless inclined, to a very considerable extent, to agree.

A person in the gallery then begged to know upon what principle boxing was excluded from the list of gymnastic exercises. He has been in the habit, personally, of practising it for many years, and was convinced of its fitness and utility.

Dr. Gilchrist said that boxing could not be permitted – it was not a social amusement.

The gentlemen in the gallery (we understand) replied that he thought it was a particularly social amusement; because less than two people could never be engaged in it.

A person in the body of the theatre observed that boxing was a practice which kept a man always alive – taught him to open his eyes.

Dr. Gilchrist – Yes and to shut those of his neighbours.

At the request of several voices in the meeting, the exercises to be adopted were then described: they consisted chiefly of leaping, climbing, running, jumping, riding the wooden horse, and throwing the javelin.

A student of Mr. Voelker's academy assured the assembly that riding the wooden horse would be of incomparable advantage to anybody who intended venturing to make the same trial on a real one.

After a good deal more speaking – a good deal of which might have been spared – the meeting broke up with great order and 'thanks' to Dr. Gilchrist. The worthy Doctor seemed to enter with immense heart into the subject; looking forward anxiously to the time when such degenerate Englishmen as now waddled about our London streets should be talked of as 'splacknucks', gone and not regretted. It really seemed as though there were but two things in the world which the Doctor regrets – the one, that he had not been stretched (by gymnastics) in his youth to the length of six feet; and the other, that he had not been born (instead of being a Doctor) to the title and estate of a dancing-master.

The Times, Thursday 23 March 1826 (v.76, p.131)

A young lady advertises in a contemporary print for a husband, and states that she will:

walk for half an hour, on next Sunday, the 26th instant, at three o'clock p.m., on the north side of Merrion-square, prepared to receive any written communication that may be handed to her. In order that she might be easily distinguished from the many other ladies who will be walking there, most of whose ultimate views in walking there and every where else are the same as the advertiser's, although differently evinced, she begs to describe her dress: *– She will wear a Leghorn bonnet, white lace veil, with a plume of white feathers, and a green silk opera* *cloak lined with white sarcenet, a swansdown muff, and a black velvet reticule with a steel clasp, which will be open to receive any billet that may, by proper dexterity, be dropped into it.*

Freeman's Journal, Monday 27 March 1826
(v.76, p.160)

∽

FLEA POWER

Mouffet relates that an ingenious English mechanic, named Mark, made a golden chain of the length of a finger, with a lock and key, which was dragged by a flea; he had heard of another that was harnessed to a golden chariot, which it drew with the greatest ease. Another English workman made an ivory coach, with six horses, a coachman on the seat, with a dog between his legs, a postillion, four persons in the coach, and four lackeys behind – which was also dragged by a single flea. At such a spectacle, one would hardly know which most to admire, the strength and agility of the insect, or the patience of the workman. Latreille mentions a flea dragging a silver cannon on wheels that was 24 times its own weight, which being charged with powder, was fired without the flea appearing alarmed.

The Wiltshire Gazette, **Thursday 30 March 1826**
(v.76, p.179)

～

RELIGION A LA MODE

An odd practice is now the fashion in Paris. The ladies of quality issue cards for an assembly in favour of the prisoners and poor. The inviter commences these good works with a sumptuous dinner, to which persons well qualified only are invited. A preacher is of course present (by the by, every lady of fashion has an hour or two's *tête-à-tête* with a priest regularly every morning during her toilet, it is the tip of fashion). After the repast, the community retire to sumptuous salon, the ladies, dressed profoundly, pour into their carriages, which fill the court-yards and the surrounding streets, the gendarmes rush about, &c. A stranger would imagine that a rout was going forward. The company arrived, a priest gives a sermon against pride, superfluities, and luxury. A collection is made, and the lady has thus the honour of being styled charitable, and at the same time (no minor honour) of displaying her elegant furniture.

The Times, **Friday 7 April 1826 (v.76, p.247)**

~

BEE WAR

A few days since, a remarkably singular and interesting exhibition of the wonderful instinctive principles of the bee occurred in this neighbourhood. It appears that a swarm of these sagacious insects, the property of a person living at Pest-house (about a mile from the town), directed their course in search of food towards the stocks of hives belonging to Mr. Rattu, an eminent gardener and florist, residing at Fratton, about a mile distant from Pest-house. It is supposed that they were invited thither by the luxurious and rich abundance of delicious sweets that the plantations of Mr. Rattu, even at this early part of the season, so temptingly affords; and especially by the production of a bed of mignonette, sown near the apiary of the occupier of the premises. It appears that a squadron or detachment of these intruders from Pest-house first made their appearance on the more reflorescent dominions of their neighbours; which intrusion was justly resented on their part by strong and vigorous opposition, and many of the depredators were killed and wounded. Those who escaped to tell the tale of this disastrous invasion hastened back to their own community; and, as is it well known that the bee is so easily irritated as to make frequent attacks, even on suspicion of intended injury, the whole body at Pest-house was speedily put in motion, and a war of extermination was declared against the innocent opposers of the late invaders. It seems that the enemy's entire force did not move towards the inhabitants at Fratton at the same time, but went over in detached bodies, and arrived at different intervals, until a mass was formed, near the mouth of the hives, of the size of a hat, consisting in number of about 7,000 or 8,000 bees! Thus congregated they were at liberty to commit their unlawful ravages upon the rightful property of others with impunity, which could not be borne with, and thereby a combat was provokingly induced. A spirited resistance having been determined on, a battle ensued for 14 successive days. The result of this conflict has proved destructive to the innocent defenders of Fratton, several thousands of them being killed, and their homes, during the fortnight of voracious contention, plundered of about two hundred weight of honey – squadrons of the depredators being constantly engaged in carrying off their blood-stained spoils. Mr. Rattu was, during the time, frequently occupied proximate to the apiary in defending his property, by a piece of wood in the shape of a battledoor.

The Times, **Monday 10 April 1826 (v.76, p.258)**

~

RECIPE FOR A LADIES'

BOARDING SCHOOL

Take a large house and garden (if with a small paddock of land so much the better) within ten miles of St. Paul's, and near the crossing of two public roads if possible. Furnish one or two rooms elegantly for receiving company, and the rest of the house as economically as you can. Take a large board, if in the form of a crescent then so much the better, for that denotes that all is right; paint upon it 'Humbug House,' or any other words of similar import, adding 'establishment for young ladies,' and if there ever has been any person of the name celebrated, add the name, but if it be Figgins, or Hitchcock, or the like, it had better be omitted. This forms what you might call the paste of the establishment. This being done, take any retired lady's maid, dismissed companion, or other female who has nothing better to do. Take also a French milliner whose face no longer charms, a dismissed musician from one of the minor theatres, a broken down clerk to teach ciphering, a philosophical cobler to give lectures, and a sign painter out of work to teach drawing; amalgamate them to a consistency; and you have the materials of an 'establishment for young ladies.' Advertise at low terms, but make out long bills for extras, allow the ladies to romp and idle the greater part of their time; but hire an unbeneficed clergyman, or newspaper reporter to prepare the holyday letters; and as for the drawings and fancy work, they are to be had best and cheapest ready-made.

The Ass, **Friday 14 April 1826 (v.76, p.285)**

~

ABOLITION OF LOTTERIES

☞ By risking a small Sum you may gain
a large Fortune in the present Lottery,
all to be decided next Wednesday, 3rd May,
being the very last but one that will ever
be offered in this Kingdom.

[NOTE: In 1826 the concerns regarding gambling
were so great that lotteries were banned, with MP
Edward Ellice expressing the opinion that 'there
might be great prizes in the lottery, but none
sufficiently great to compensate the credulity of the
public'. (*The Examiner*, Sunday 20 March 1825).
Lotteries were reinstated in 1994, and now achieve
sales of over five billion pounds a year.]

Advertisement, 1826 (v.77, p.15)

~

CAFE DE L'EUROPE

Wine, Coffee, and Reading Room
The proprietor of this splendid coffee room, which
is fitted up, not only with Taste and Elegance, but
with a view to the comforts of its frequenters, has
for his object the supply of every description of
European wines.

REFRESHMENTS

	s.	d.
Tea, &c.	1	3
Ditto, with Eggs	1	6
Coffee	1	3
Cup of Coffee	0	6
Ditto with roll or muffin	0	9
Sandwiches	0	6
Ditto anchovies	0	8
Ditto shrimps	0	8
Anchovy toast	0	6

Negus, lemonade, orgeat, & jellies
Soda water and ginger beer.

To render this Establishment worthy the Patronage of the Public, Morning and Evening Newspapers, French and German Journals, with the most popular French and English Periodicals and Pamphlets will be provided; and the Waiters speak the French and German Languages.

Advertisement, 1826 (v.77, p.36)

∼

GOOD COATS AND

GOOD LOOKS

In a case tried lately in the Common Pleas, the plaintiff sought to recover damages of a Police-officer for having seized him in the street at noon, on an unfounded suspicion of felony. Mr. Serjeant Wilde, for the defence, argued that his client could not tell the respectability of the plaintiff, as he was no better dressed than his own workmen. Judge Best said, 'If the plaintiff's appearance was such as to give him reasonable grounds to suspect that he had stolen property about him, he was authorised to detain him until convinced to the contrary.' A man's appearance at noon, on the streets, becomes a matter of serious consideration. Lawyers are fond of definitions, and it is really of the highest importance that Judge Best should define when a man's dress becomes sufficiently shabby to give him that appearance that allows Police-officers to seize him on suspicion of felony. We know some noble and honourable members whose infirm looks and shabby coats may bring them into jeopardy. We advise the ear of W—— to wash his face and hands, and order a new suit of clothes.

The Examiner, Sunday 15 July 1827 (v.77, p.308)

Mr. Davis, the highly talented artist, lately returned from Rome, and now resident in this city, has sent to the Picture Gallery a pleasing proof of his abilities in No. 74, *Il Biglietto di Amore*. It represents a country girl of the neighbourhood of Rome, dictating a letter to one of the Itinerant Secretaries of Cupid (or indeed, any other of 'the powers that be' willing and able to pay such scribes for epistolary assistance) who are easily to be found in the public places of 'the Eternal City.' The figure of the Contradina is very graceful, and her attire somewhat more than sufficiently elegant, considering that the handsome peasant can neither read nor write. There is much cheerful archness and a sylph-like form in the yet younger female companion of the love-sick damsel. And the bearded sage of amorous philosophy, mending his pen, and drily listening to the soft tale he is about to indite, exhibits a countenance finely fraught with expression.

(From *The Norwich Gazette*)
***The Morning Chronicle*, Tuesday 21 October 1828 (v.80, p.22)**

LONDON FEMALE

FASHIONS FOR NOVEMBER:

A DINNER DRESS

A dress of fawn-coloured satin, with two deep flounces round the border, set on rather scanty. Each of these flounces is edged by a broad wadded rouleau, over which are entwined, obliquely, ornaments representing date leaves; each leaf of the green of that foliage, edged by silk, the same colour as the dress. The corsage is made tight to the shape, with a Circassian drapery folding over the bust: this drapery is gathered up at each shoulder in a novel and elegant manner, and from where it is drawn together depend ornaments which form mancherons over the sleeves, which are of a moderate fullness. A hat of white gros de Naples, with an ornament, and rosette under the brim, of gauze ribbon, most beautifully brocaded, from whence depend strings of the same, forms the head dress. The crown is splendidly adorned with three detached bouquets of flowers, consisting of the guilder-rose, the red, and the maiden's-blush rose; and beautiful species of fruiting. The ear-pendants are of finely wrought gold; and round the throat, but not lower, are two rows of valuable oriental pearls, from whence depends a convent-cross of the same. The shoes are of fawn-coloured gros de Naples, but the ribbon which ties them, *en sandals*, is white.

The Morning Chronicle, Friday 31 October 1828 (v.80, p.48)

~

GENTLEMEN'S FASHIONS

FOR NOVEMBER

SHOOTING COSTUME

A Mexican jacket of bottle-green, with pockets on the sides, and sugar-loaf buttons, and under waistcoat of black silk, grey breaches of knit thread, very full long gaiters of yellow leather fastened with buckles. A cap of grey cloth, made with a front, en visor, of black leather; a silk cravat, tied carelessly.

ADDITIONAL NOVELTIES IN GENTLEMEN'S DRESS

The cut of the coats has varied little; the sleeves are less ample, but the coat flaps and the collars, turning back, are wide: the collar seems to float as it turns back, but the lining, which used formerly to stiffen it, is exploded.

A dancer, whose coat does not fall back from off the shoulders, and every part au gré des Vents, would be regarded as an intruder in every dancing room of fashion.

The buttons on coats are set nearer to each other than formerly.

In morning deshabille some dashers are seen with pantaloons of grey kerseymere, and stockings of the same colour.

A man of taste, who wishes to wear his hair according to the newest fashions, should have it almost shorn on the temples, very long on the summit of the head, but so arranged as to discover the whole of the forehead.

***The Morning Chronicle*, Friday 31 October 1828 (v.80, p.48)**

~

ADDITIONAL NOVELTIES

IN GENTLEMEN'S DRESS

The *Dandies'* magazine for the present month contains a list of alterations in the costumes of the things which perambulate the town under the denomination of *gentle-men* –

'A very striking revolution, and which will form a striking revolution in the annals of fashion, has taken place since last month, which is suffering the beard to grow. It is true, that last autumn we beheld mustachios on the lips of those dandies who belonged to the most quiet professions; *favourites* were added about the middle of winter, under the chin, and now all the chin looks as if it called for the razor.'

Scroggins, in his *Magasin des Modes*, seems to have adopted the spirit of the *Dandies'* magazine, for he says –

'A very dirty revolution has taken place in the *features* of the fashionables, who no longer wear whiskers, but have adopted the full length beard of a *mourning smochee*, a circumstance which has excited the attentions of the Sheffield razor-makers, many of whom have been thrown out of employment. The barbers too, except those employed in making chin-wigs, are very indignant.'

The Observer, Sunday 26 April 1829
(v.82, p.67)

~

ANSWERS TO

CORRESPONDENTS

A lays a wager to a considerable amount with B that there is NOT a housekeeper in Newgate-street; B says there is. Who wins?

*** This is one of those catch-wagers which ought NOT to be paid: there is a Mr. NOTT in Newgate-street.

A bets B a goose will travel further than a turkey. Which wins?

*** We should back the goose, as the turkey will not travel by night.

Bell's Life in London, Sunday 2 November 1828
(v.80, p.62)

Stephen Stacey is one of the unfortunate men who were so dreadfully mangled by a leopard a few weeks ago in Oxford. The accident alluded to happened in the following manner: – While the den in which the animal was confined was being painted, a quantity of paint fell accidentally on the leopard, and one of the keepers ignorantly applying turpentine to remove the paint, the dreadful state of agony and irritation consequently produced by the application caused him to turn upon his keepers, one of whom, Stacey, he lacerated dreadfully in the scalp, while his companion was so seriously mangled that he at present lies in a dangerous state.

(From *The Windsor Express*)
The Morning Chronicle, Monday 2 November 1828 (v.80, p.77)

~

MARVELLOUS ADVENTURES

At Preston County Court, last Wednesday, an action was tried, brought by a person named Pacy, against a pound-keeper named Ramage, for damages done by a cow, which the defendant had allowed to escape from the pound. It appeared by the evidence, that on the evening of the 8th of July, the cow was found running about the streets, to the terror of the passengers, for which she was impounded. She had not been long in duress when, having mounted six stone steps, she got into a passage, by forcing open a door at the end of which, she gained admittance into a room where the pound-keeper's wife and some friends were taking tea, who, on the appearance of their visitor, made a hasty retreat. The pound-keeper and his assistants soon brought the runaway back to prison, and locked her up, as they thought, for the night; but on visiting the pound next morning, it was found she had again escaped, and it was ascertained that she had climbed a heap of stones in the corner of the yard, by which she gained the top of a wall 12 feet high, along which she must have walked 10 feet, though it was but a brick and a half thick, where she got on top of a shed, on which she walked, till coming to a sky-light over a file-cutter's shop, who was at work below, her foot went through the glass with a crash that, added to the appearance of the cloven foot, terrified the poor file-cutter, who ran off with the horrible feeling in his mind that the Majesty of the Cloven Foot had come to pay him a visit. The visitor, however, soon extricated her foot, and continued her wanderings, increasing her elevation, whenever it was practicable, till she reached the roof of an old building used as a cotton store, at the height of a three-storey house. This roof proving too weak to support the unusual weight, gave way, and she fell through, and was found the next morning in the upper room of the store, very much injured by the night's adventure. The owner of the cow was obliged to pay 2*l.* 2*s.* to the owner of the store, for the damage done to his roof, and brought his action against the pound-keeper to recover back that sum. – The Jury returned a verdict for the plaintiff for the sum claimed.

The Morning Chronicle, **Saturday 8 December 1828 (v.80, p.113)**

BOW-STREET – Eliza Merchant, a black-eyed girl, of that class of women known as 'unfortunates,' was charged by Garnet Comerford, a sailor, with robbing him of four sovereigns, several dollars and half-crowns, and his shoes. The tar stated that on Wednesday evening, about eight o'clock, he left the house of his Captain, the honourable Mr. Duncan, at the west end of town, intending to pay a visit to a sister, whom he had not seen since he left England in the Seringapatem. On the way, he met as tight a looking frigate as ever he clapt his eyes on. She hoisted friendly colours; he hove to; and they agreed together to steer into port. They sailed up the Strand, when she said she would tow him to a snug berth, and he should share her hammock for the night. He consented; and when he awoke in the morning he found that she had cut and run. His rigging had been thrown all about the room, his four sovereigns and silver, and shoes were carried off.

The Morning Chronicle, **Saturday 8 December 1828 (v.80, p.113)**

~

VOLTAIRE'S PILE OINTMENT

Prepared from cooling and emollient Herbs, gives instantaneous relief, and cures after a very few dressings the most painful kind of Piles. Sold in pots, with directions, at 2*s*. 9*d*. and 4*s*. 6*d*. each, by W. Stirling, 86, High-street, Whitechapel; and may be had of Sanger, 150, Oxford-street; and Barclay, Fleet-market.

Bell's Life in London, **Sunday 4 January 1829 (v.81, p.97)**

~

A DAMP SWEAT

Holt, the officer of Chorlston-row, during his perambulations on Friday last, met a lad who appeared to have a copious perspiration trickling down his face, and anxious to know what had brought it on, he stopped him, and taking off his hat, found it contained in it a woman's gown, wringing wet, the dew from which had caused the appearance which Holt had imagined was the result of some powerful sudorific. The gown had been abstracted a few minutes before from the washing mug of a woman in the neighbourhood, for which the magistrates on Saturday committed the lad to the sessions.

Egan's Weekly Courier, Sunday 19 April 1829
(v.82, p.33)

~

AFFECTIONATE AND

SAGACIOUS GOOSE

Mr. Burnett, Craigelluchie Inn, Elgin, has a goose, nearly a year old, which has formed so strong an attachment towards him as to follow him any distance, and through the crowds and bustle of High-street. A few days since the kindly animal followed him down the street and into a hair dresser's shop, where it patiently waited until its master got shaved, after which it accompanied him on another visit into the shop of a friend, and then proceeded home with him. The goose is so well acquainted with Mr. Burnett that it readily recognises him in whatever dress he may appear. It even knows his voice when he is not to be seen, and no sooner does he speak than it responds to him in its own unintelligible dialect.

Egan's Weekly Courier, **Sunday 19 April 1829**
(v.82, p.33)

❖

It has been calculated that the total number of copies of newspapers printed in Great Britain, during the week, is nearly 500,000; that the daily average is consequently more than 70,000; and that, including children and others who cannot read, every 157 persons have one newspaper between them.

[NOTE: In 2010 something over 12 million papers were sold each day, which, with a population of over 60 million (including children and those who cannot read), means that every five persons had a paper between them.]

Birmingham Journal, **Saturday 25 April 1829**
(v.82, p.45)

~

NOVEL REWARD

A society of antiquated ladies, at Paris, are stated to have offered a reward of 5000 francs to the inventor of a substance to keep their wigs fast on their heads. They are said to have been induced to make this offer in consequence of one of their members having recently had the lamentable misfortune to have her wig knocked off into the pit at the theatre.

Birmingham Journal, **Saturday 25 April 1829**
(v.82, p.45)

~

WINE

The rage for superannuated wine is one of the most ridiculous vulgar errors of modern epicurism. 'The bee's wing,' 'thick crust,' 'loss of strength,' &c. which wine fanciers consider the beauty of their tawny favourite, 'fine old port,' are forbidding manifestations of decomposition, and of the departure of some of the best qualities of the wine. – *Kitchener* – Wines bottled in good order may be fit to drink in six months (especially if bottled in October) but they are not in perfection before twelve. From that to two years they may continue so, but it would be improper to keep them longer.

Birmingham Journal, **Saturday 2 May 1829**
(v.82, p.70)

~

TRUE ENGLISH FEELING

A butcher in the vicinity of the Commercial-road, a few days ago killed an ox, and sent part of the beef and a quantity of the suet to his son-in-law, a weaver in Bethnal-green, who hung it up so near to the window, that some one in the night broke a pane of glass and carried off the suet. Yesterday morning the weaver, missing his suet, went to a public-house in the neighbourhood, where he posted up the following notice, which still remains in evidence of the right John Bull generosity and spirit:

'Whereas last night a quantity of beef suet was taken away from the house of James Henry Woodford – this is to give notice that if the person who took it away will appear, and prove that he was forced to do so by distress, the same James Henry Woodford will give him half a dozen pounds of flour to make the suet into dumplings, but if he cannot prove that he was in distress when he stole it, the said James Henry Woodford will fight him, and give him five shillings, if he beats him.'

Bell's Life in London, Sunday 3 May 1829 (v.82, p.78)

To the Editor of *Bell's Life in London*

Anatomical Subjects

Sir,

In consequence of a severe indisposition in my breeches pocket, I have for some days been confined to bread and – I shudder while I write the word – *water*; and having time to reflect, I have turned my attention to the good of the country. Among other *subjects* that occupy the attention of Parliament, the *subject* of supplying *subjects* to the surgeons is not the least interesting; and as it is a *subject* of national importance, every hint given by the *subjects* of this realm must be valuable. Permit me, then, to suggest, that, as upon a principle of reciprocity, 'where good is gained good ought to be returned,' the most advisable plan for securing a constant supply of good *subjects* would be to make it a *sina qua non*, that all Parsons having a plurality of livings, and all of the same class having benefices exceeding 1,000*l.* a year, should be permitted to hold these good things only upon condition that their carcasses should be given for the benefit of science, and of course, for the benefit of those individuals from the tenths of whose hard industry they reap such signal advantages. This, I think, would be coming to the point at once; but if it should be thought to consign too many of these 'fat and lazy drones' to the knife, why then, let us have tithe for tithe, and let it be enacted that in return for our tenth we have one tenth of these 'wolves in sheep's clothing,' exempting Curates under 100*l.* a year, and embracing the whole Bench of Bishops.

Yours &c. Jack Scroggins

Bell's Life in London, Sunday 10 May 1829
(v.82, p.103)

~

EXPERIENTA DOCIT

There is nothing like having Members of Parliament well versed on all subjects; although the experience of an Honourable Member was on Tuesday last somewhat oddly declared. On a motion that the Juvenile Offenders' Bill be committed, Mr. Pearse rose and said, with the most praiseworthy gravity, 'I think the bill is indispensable – I strenuously advocate the system of whipping: *from my own experience* I am able to say whipping has the best effect on offenders!'

    ***The Liberal*, Sunday 17 May 1829 (v.82, p.112)**

PATENT Detonating walking-stick gun

J. Lang begs to inform Noblemen and Gentlemen that he has just obtained the express privilege of manufacturing the above gun, which is on an entirely new principle. The top draws out similar to a telescope, and bends, which forms a stock which can be used with the greatest facility. A rifle barrel can be used with the same gun, which, for rabbit and rook shooting, makes it one of the most complete things of the kind ever seen in this country. – To be seen and had at Lang's Gun Repository, 7, Haymarket, adjoining the Shooting Gallery.

[NOTE: A walking stick that doubled as a gun was, of course, a handy invention – with highwaymen, footpads and rascals on the prowl, who wouldn't want a little light ordnance for the road? There were, however, drawbacks to a weapon that went everywhere with you. Certainly, an accidental discharge could be mortifying. *Jackson's Oxford*

Journal reported, on Saturday 26 May 1832, an episode of rook shooting that went badly awry for Laurence Smith, Esq., who had not only his hat but also a portion of his scalp removed when the light trigger that such weapons possessed was unexpectedly brushed during conversation. *The Examiner* of Sunday 14 September 1839 repeats an account of a gentleman passing along the York Road with 'a walking-stick gun under one arm, and the muzzle end behind him, the instrument happening to slip down, he gave it a sharp jerk up; and probably owing to the lock rubbing against his arm, it went off, and the contents lodged in the lower part of the body of a man who happened to be walking behind him at the time'.]

Bell's Life in London, Sunday 17 May 1829
(v.82, p.123)

Mr. James Blaze, landlord of the Turk's Head, in Harley-street, was on Friday fined 5*l.* at the Mary-la-bonne office for allowing the game of 'Bumble-puppy' to be played in his house.

Bell's Life in London, Sunday 17 May 1829 (v.82, p.128)

MULTUM IN PARVO

Publicans must be cautious in allowing any games on their premises – two landlords were fined £5 each on Friday for allowing 'bumble-puppy' and 'bagatelle' to be played.

Birmingham Journal, Saturday 23 May 1829 (v.82, p.155)

At Worship-street, an information was laid against the host of the Three Jolly Weavers, for permitting dominoes to be played in his house; but it appearing the men were merely playing for the pot of beer they were drinking, the information was dismissed.

[NOTE: Bumble-puppy was a name normally given to a version of whist, although it was sometimes also used to describe ninepins or bagatelle. 'Laying an information' is the action of informing a magistrate that a person has committed a certain offence – in this case allowing gambling to occur in licensed premises. There would often be a payment given to an informer, some of whom made a living from the practice.]

***Bell's Life in London*, Sunday 28 June 1829 (v.82, p.178)**

Another tremendous fire occurred on Wednesday – the whole of that immense building, the Royal Bazaar, in Oxford-street, was consumed in the short space of an hour. Scarcely an article has been saved, and independently of the destruction of the edifice, by no means covered by insurance, the loss of property to the poor tenants of the standings has been grievous. The fire was occasioned by an attempt to produce a picturesque effect of the conflagration at York Minster – nothing could have been more successful.

John Bull, **Sunday 31 May 1829 (v.82, p.131)**

$\sim$

REMEDY FOR CONSUMPTION

A French professor, M. Cruveillier, has recommended smoking the leaves of the Belladonna, for its soothing effects in cases of consumption, and as a practice which he has found to be attended with beneficial results. The leaves are first infused in a strong solution of opium, and dried imperfectly in the same manner as tobacco. The patient begins with two pipes a day, and increases by degrees to five or six in the same time. It is probable that the efficacy of this remedy consists in the combination of narcotic principles, and not in the mode of its administration; it might be better were it used in the form of aqueous vapours, as a more convenient mode of application, especially in the cases of females and children, and as free from the objection of having, simultaneously with the calming principle of fumigation, an empyreumatic oil, which might counteract its beneficial effects.

Birmingham Journal, **Saturday 13 June 1829**
(v.82, p.149)

~

METROPOLITAN

NEW POLICE

The district of which the new police force take charge, at the outset, will be a very extensive one: it will include the following parishes:– viz. St. James, Westminster; St. Martin-in-the-Fields; St. George, Hanover-square; St. Margaret and St. John the Evangelist; St. Paul, Covent-garden; St. Mary-le-Strand; St. Clement Danes; St. Anne, Soho; St. Mary-le-bone; St. Giles-in-the-Fields; St. George, Bloomsbury; St. Andrew, Holborn; St. George the Martyr. The district including the parishes above mentioned will be divided into five divisions, each division under the charge of a superior officer, named a superintendent of police, to whom it is proposed to allot a salary of 200*l.* per annum. The total amount of force for the whole of the five divisions will not fall short of 800 men. The men employed will be divided into four classes: the superintendent, above mentioned; the inspector at a salary of 100*l.* per annum; the police serjeant, with pay at the rate of 3*s.* 6*d.* a day; the ordinary police constable, with pay at the rate of 3*s.* per diem. – No man will be accepted for the role of police constable, who is not of a vigorous constitution, who is above 35 years of age, and under five feet seven inches in height. – The commissioners require that the whole time of each man employed shall be devoted to the service.

Sunday Times, Sunday 16 August 1829
(v.83, p.17)

~

THE NEW POLICE FORCE

The Commissioners of the Metropolitan Police sit daily in an apartment at the Home Office, and are in constant communication with Mr. Peel. The men, we understand, are to be on duty both night and day, and are to be relieved at stated hours – to be alternately engaged sixteen hours out of the four-and-twenty on one day, and eight hours the other. They are all to wear a uniform costume – blue frock-coats, with white metal buttons, bearing the words, 'Metropolitan Police Force.' A straight sword, a broad black belt round their waists, and a brass plate bearing their number. In addition to this, they will carry a small, turned staff of authority.

Birmingham Journal, Saturday 22 August 1829 (v.83, p.25)

MIDDLESEX SESSIONS – Saturday, Oct. 31.

A great number of petty assault cases were tried this morning, and the offenders, in almost every instance, were either acquitted or sentenced to pay a small fine and be discharged. In some instances the prosecutors preferred indictments at once in this Court; but the great many were commitments from the Police-offices. The chairman very properly censured the practice of sending such cases for trial, and observed, that since the discretionary power of the Magistrates was so much increased, they ought never to have left the Police-office.

A female prosecutor, in one indictment, asserted as her reason for not going first to the Police-office, that 'There was no good to be got out of *those old washerwoman* at the Police-offices;' and, unquestionably, if the charges to-day are to be taken as a sample of their method of doing business, they well deserved the appellation which the spleen of this virago bestowed on them.

John Bull, **Sunday 25 October 1829**
(v.83, p.222)

~

THE NEW POLICE

At the wardmote of Farringdon Without, held on Monday, a vote of thanks was unanimously passed to the New Police, for the extreme activity they exhibited at the late fire in Fetter Lane; where their conduct was most favourably contrasted with that of the dozing drunken vagabonds of the City watch. A vote on the censure of the latter was proposed, but withdrawn.

The Spectator, **Saturday 1 May 1830 (v.85, p.9)**

~

THE POPULACE AND

THE NEW POLICE

The strong feeling which exists towards the New Police caused a serious disturbance on Tuesday at the west end of the town. When the King returned from the House of Lords, loud shouts were raised of – 'Down with the New Police!' 'No Martial Law!' Shortly after his majesty alighted, two of the police took two pick-pockets into custody at the corner of St. James's-street, when the mob immediately attacked the policemen and shouted – 'Rescue for the prisoners!' A number of policemen arrived to the assistance of their comrades, and a general riot then ensued. The mob proceeded to the house of Messrs. Hibbert, manufacturers of the policemen's clothing, in Pall-mall, where they broke the windows and did other damage.

Birmingham Journal, Saturday 6 November 1830 (v.85, p.314)

~

THE NEW POLICE

By an official return made last week, it appears that from the 1st of January 1831, to the 1st of January 1832, the new police force has apprehended no less than 72,824 persons, on different charges, viz: 45,907 males, and 26,917 females. Out of this number, 2,955 were committed for trial; 21,843 were summarily convicted before the Magistrates; 24,239 were discharged by the Magistrates; and 23,787 drunken characters were discharged by the Superintendants of the police at the station-house, after they became sober. The number of persons charged before the magistrates for being drunk were 7,566; of this number 3,187 were discharged, and 4,379 were fined 5s. each, which would amount to 1,094l. 15s.; of the number fined, 3,187 were males, and 1,194 were females. By the return it appears that the greatest number of persons were apprehended for drunkenness in the months of December and July, and the least number in February. From the above returns the police have apprehended on an average about 199 per day.

[NOTE: In his book *Police Ethics: Crisis in Law Enforcement* Tom Barker reports that in the first two years of the Metropolitan Police

3,200 new constables left the force, two-thirds of them dismissed for drunkenness.]

The Observer, Sunday 8 April 1832
(v.90, p.155)

The Duke of Gloucester has regularly conveyed to each theatre he may please visit his *tea equipage*, and the Duchess of St. Albans, in imitation of Royalty, has adopted the same plan. – There are rooms attached to the private boxes occupied by these personages, where the *hissing-urn* or more humble *tea-kettle* are put into requisition.

Sunday Times, Sunday 16 August 1829
(v.83, p.18)

A correspondent in the *Lancet* mentions a curious cure for hydrophobia, namely, of dividing the bitten part, throwing a pinch of gunpowder into the wound, and then blowing it up! This practice is said to have been adopted by Colonel Gatacre, of Gatacre Park, Shropshire, with complete success.

Birmingham Journal, Saturday 22 August 1829
(v.83, p.25)

~

TIGHT LACING

Another instance of the folly and fatal effects of the following, for the sake of appearances only, the fashion of the day, has occurred in the practice of Mr. Prowse, of Bristol. The subject of this notice was an interesting female, of about twenty years of age, who was in the constant habit of lacing so tightly that she could not even stoop in the ordinary way; and was generally so much distressed as to be obliged to loosen her stays whenever she returned home. This unfortunate habit brought on cough, violent palpitation, and other diseases of the heart, which terminated in a premature death. The facts in this case were fully substantiated by a post mortem examination. The cavity of the chest was found to be considerably reduced in size, caused, in the first instance, by the external and excessive pressure of the stays, and afterwards rendered permanent by the adhesion of the whole of the surface of the lungs to the internal surface of the membrane (pleura) covering the inside of the ribs.

[NOTE: The health problems stemming from the use of corsets were clear in the early nineteenth century, although the explanations given were not always accurate. In 1829 *The Leicester Chronicle* ventured: 'Where tight lacing is practised, young women from 15 to 20 years of age are found so dependent upon their corsets that they faint whenever they lay them aside. For as soon as the thorax and abdomen are relaxed, by being deprived of their usual support, the blood rushing downwards, in consequence of the diminished resistance to its motion, empties the vessels of the head, and thus occasions fainting.' (Saturday 30 May 1829)]

Birmingham Journal, Saturday 22 August 1829
(v.83, p.30)

～

FREAKS OF THE MOON

The York Herald *gravely gives the following under the head of Celestial Phenomena:*

A person has called at our office, who relates some very curious appearances which, he says, (in company with several others) were witnessed in the moon, on the road from Leeds to this city, on Thursday night. When they came near Halton Bar, about 11 o'clock, the moon had just risen above the horizon, and was shining serenely in a clear atmosphere. As the party were remarking to each other on the fineness of the night, the moon seemed to part in two, its disc separating down the centre, and leaving an apparent space of about one yard between the two hemispheres, in which the distant and deep azure of the sky was visible. Whilst in this state, from the northern limb of the lunar orb, a bright appearance darted forth in form like the head of a spear, and surrounded with brilliant stars. On a sudden, it seemed to be withdrawn, and in its place appeared the distinct forms of two human figures, which were visible to the waist, and one arm and the hand of one of them was extended on the surface of that half of the disc from which it emerged. A deep red girdle was round the head of one of them. This appearance remained for some time, when a cloud obscured the moon altogether from view. On its having passed away, the same occurrence was renewed, and our informant states that the whole time, during which he had an uninterrupted view of these strange phenomena, was above an hour, and that he and those that were with him were greatly amazed at the wonderful appearance. We give this account as nearly as possible as it was related to us, and no doubt some one may have seen these phenomena, and may be able to give a more scientific description, and perhaps definition of them.

Birmingham Journal, c. **Saturday 29 August 1829**
(v.83, p.48)

~

THE FIRE KING

On Friday the Fire King exhibited before a number of spectators, and made an extraordinary change in his wonderful performances. He began by washing his hands in molten lead, and his mouth with boiling oil. He was proceeding to swallow his usual dose of phosphorous, when a gentleman from the father end of the room, Mr. Cooper, a chymist, of Exeter, called to him to take a tea-spoonful of prussic acid in its stead. The Fire King agreed, but said he should take his antidote first, for which purpose he retired for a few minutes. On his return he was proceeding to fill a tea-spoonful from his own phial, but Mr. Cooper produced one from his pocket, to which his majesty did not object; and after having in vain requested Mr. Cooper, and several other gentlemen, to administer the dose, he knelt down on one knee, and deliberately swallowed the tea-spoonful, the spectators regarding him with awful apprehension. He instantly jumped on his feet; for a moment he staggered, and appeared unable to stand, his eyes rolling frightfully in his head. The spectators were horror-struck – it was but the feeling of a moment. The Fire King appeared to make a sort of convulsive effort, and instantly assured them all danger was at an end. The burst of applause that followed testified the interest felt by all present. He said, in reply to inquiries, that on first swallowing the poison he felt stupefied; and also felt an extraordinary sensation in his temples and eyes, but it was soon gone, and left only a heaviness behind. He then said that he would take half a spoonful more; but there was a general cry, 'indeed you shall not.' A gentleman suggested that the poison should be tried on some animal, a proposal which, unfortunately for Mr. Welch's cat, was instantly agreed to. The poor cat was speedily caught and introduced to the company, when a medical gentleman cautiously administered four drops from the same phial from which his Majesty had taken his quantum. In a few seconds the poor cat had become convulsed, and for about half a minute it uttered the most piercing cries; its convulsions became gradually fainter, and in less than a minute and a half its life was extinct. The King then took 21 grains of phosphorous, after which he would have taken half an ounce of exalic acid, had not the company prevented him. It was mentioned in the room that M. Chabert has discovered a remedy for hydrophobia, and intends to have himself bit by a mad dog, for the purpose of proving the efficacy of his remedy.

The Observer, Sunday 1 November 1829
(v.83, p.225)

~

PHRENOLOGY

The *Scotsman* gives an account of a visit paid by Mr. Combe to the Richmond Lunatic Asylum in Dublin, accompanied by Dr. Crawford. It seems that Dr. Crawford had written down the characteristic features of several cases of insanity, and he proposed that Mr. Combe should examine the heads of the patients, deliver his opinion on them, and afterwards have the written notes compared with Mr. Combe's remarks. We select the following as specimens of the judgment obtained by the two different means. On the head of E.S. Mr. Combe remarked, 'This is the worst head I ever saw. The combination is worse than Hare's – Combativeness and destructiveness are fearfully large, and the moral organs altogether very deficient: Benevolence is the best-developed of them, but it is fearfully small when compared with combativeness and destructiveness. I am surprised that this man was not executed before he became insane.' Dr. Crawford gave the following account of this unhappy person: 'Patient E.S. aged 34. Ten years since first admission. Total want of moral feeling and principle, leading to the indulgence of every vice, and to the commission even of *crime*. Considerable intelligence, ingenuity, and plausibility; a scourge to his family from childhood, turned out of the army as an incorrigible villain; attempted the life of a soldier; repeatedly flogged; has since attempted to poison his father.' On the head of Ann Kelly, Mr. Combe observed: 'The characteristic organs are self-esteem and love of approbation, as one combination, and constructiveness, imitation, and idility, as another.' Dr. Crawford wrote, 'Monomania. Pride. Imagines she is Napoleon. Very irascible, but easily calmed by a little praise. Dresses partly as a man. Speaks of herself as a man, and in the third person. Has made herself trowsers and a highly-ornamented cloak with simple threads. Will never wear a cap.'

The Examiner, **Sunday 8 November 1829 (v.83, p.248)**

A new invention for the speedy and certain application of leeches is announced. It is made with brass wire, much of the form and size of a bell. The leeches, having great antipathy to brass wire, attach themselves to the skin, and, in general, immediately commence the operation of puncturing and suction.

Birmingham Journal, Saturday 28 November 1829
(v. 83, p.179)

~

LONDON IN NOVEMBER

Fogs, the November blessings of London, have arrived. People forced or foolish enough to quit their houses after dark have been run over, or run against; coaches driven with lamps burning in noon day have navigated the city, and coaches without lamps at night have been driven into shop windows in the Strand; gentlemen of high respectability have found themselves walking into houses of no respectability at all, and the police have been catching each other in escaping from the weather. The streets are one mass of ice and slippery mud; horses are sprawling in every direction, carts upset, and coaches broken down; every body is getting out of the misery as fast as they can, and Brighton is filling to repletion.

Birmingham Journal, Saturday 28 November 1829 (v.83, p.282)

~

EQUAL JUSTICE

Henry Edgar Kearry was indicted at the London Sessions, on Wednesday, for an assault on Mr. Astell, the East India Director. Kearry, it will be recollected, having made an application to Mr. Astell, and being haughtily repulsed, gave Mr. Astell a knock on the nose with his umbrella. Kearry was sentence to *six months' imprisonment!* On the same day, Thomas Eaton was indicted at the Surrey Sessions, for beating, bruising, and all but murdering a poor female named Leary. Leary has been in the hospital ever since the assault (3d March), and is not expected to ever to recover her wonted strength. *Eaton was fined ten pounds!!* On the same day, a fashionably dressed man, named Michael Pressford, was charged with using the most abominable language towards, and with assaulting in a violent and most indecent way, a respectable female in Blackfriars-road. The Union Hall Magistrates *fined Pressford two pounds!!!* These are three fair specimens of indifferent justice.

The Spectator, Saturday 1 May 1830 (v.85, p.10)

∿

DUTCH SPORTS

An amusement, very singular in its nature, is kept up at Namur annually. The young men of the two parts of the town, called the old and the new, assemble before the town-house, mounted on stilts, and, having marshalled themselves in two opposing battalions under regular leaders, commence a contest of the most extraordinary kind; each party endeavouring, by the exertions of the elbows and legs of the combatants, to drive back the other. The engagement sometimes continues for several hours, while the female relatives of the contending parties cheer on and encourage them in their exertions. It is said that Peter the Great, of Russia, took particular delight in being a spectator to this strange combat; as also, that one of the Dukes of Burgundy exempted the brewers from the payment of excise, in testimony of the pleasure it afforded him.

Bell's Life in London, Sunday 6 June 1830 (v.85, p.66)

~

CHIN MUSIC

On Friday we were favoured with a private view of a curious phenomenon at the Egyptian Hall. M. Boai, a German, exhibited his skill in imitating different musical sounds by striking his chin with his hands, and produced by no means an unpleasing effect. He is enabled to cause a variety of sounds which certainly are not unmusical, and in some instances the effect is somewhat similar to a rapid passage on the piano, except that the tones are not so full. He played several airs, with and without accompaniment, and was much applauded. Among the company we noticed Miss. Stephens, Mr. Sinclair, and several other persons well known in the musical world.

Bell's Life in London, Sunday 6 June 1830 (v.85, p.66)

~

A CHOICE OF EVILS

A man charged with marrying two wives declared he would rather be transported than live with either of them.

The Age, Sunday 13 June 1830 (v.85, p.79)

~

THE SIAMESE BROTHERS

We beg to call the attention of our fellow-townsmen to the exhibition at the Shakespeare Rooms of these interesting strangers. Although two remarkable well-formed bodies, possessing in every limb muscular power and energy of no common order; the singular junction at their breast bones appears to produce a surprising oneness of feeling and action, without any apparent expression, or communication of thought from one to another. – We took some pains to ascertain if each was actuated by distinct operations, but this we were unable satisfactorily to determine, so perfectly do they agree in sentiment on all subjects. An opinion expressed by Chang is invariably approved by Eng, and *vice versa*. When they rise to walk no person can discover which first felt the inclination to move; their attentions are generally directed to the same objects – have the same fancies and distastes – enjoy the same recreations – eat the same quantity and kind of food, and fall asleep and awaken simultaneously. Thus judging from the difficulty of finding in society two individuals who, in their taste, feelings, and disposition are so agreed, as at all times to prevent a collision of opinions, we are led to imagine that these interesting young men either have but one vital principle, or that their connecting link is the medium of some powerful and instantaneous communication from one to the other, which it is impossible to define. It is delightful to witness their manifest cheerful and unrestrained demeanour, and to observe that what would generally be thought conducive to inconvenience and peevishness, in their case produces perfect ease and unalloyed contentment. Such, however, is the wisdom of providence.

[NOTE: Chang and Eng, the original Siamese twins, were hugely popular, though not all of their impersonators achieved such concord: 'Greenwich was yesterday a scene of great animation and gaiety. The fair attracted much company, who enjoyed the amusements until a late hour. Every arrangement was made to preserve order, and the frolics of the fair presented a succession of entertainments, not being the less acceptable from being highly grotesque and ludicrous. Two boys were exhibited, said to be united like the Siamese twins, between whom a quarrel was excited by one of the spectators, when in the height of passion they broke their band and proceeded to fight one another, but were soon separated by the police.' (*Jackson's Oxford Journal*, Saturday 5 June 1830)]

**Birmingham Journal, Saturday 26 June 1830
(v.85, p.104)**

∼

THE ROYAL ELEPHANT

– We extract the following elegant effusion from a Dublin paper of Monday.
We rejoice to see a good house, but cannot help mourning over our present prostrate condition

of dramatic taste, when we see the proboscis of an elephant invested with a power of attraction which is denied to the superior (we do not use the word comparatively) conceptions of a Sheridan or a Goldsmith. It is lamentable. The sagacious quadruped collected in the theatre, on Saturday evening, a splendid circle of admirers, and went through her wonted movements in capital style. She failed, however, to attend to one of Shakespeare's most pointed admonitions, and said 'more than was set down for her.' The circumstance is novel, and we shall merely hint at it: immediately after the banquet scene, when the royal gormandizer has devoured five or six courses, and quaffed a cooper or so of Cham (sham!) paign, she proceeded to go through her usual pas seul. The two young attendants on the Princess Indomara (Miss. Chalmers) who, by the way, did the little she had to do on this occasion well, were moving about in all the poetry of motion to pass the sash under the elephant's feet, when lo! The giant of the forest paused, and after giving a partial elevation to one of her hinder feet, yielded to one of those imperative mandates of nature, which the sagacity of our readers will at once comprehend! In a moment, a sound was heard like the falls of Niagara, or the Cataract of the Ganges – and the stage presented every appearance of an *overflow*! The ladies covered their faces with their fans and veils – the gentlemen tittered – and the whole court of Siam was thrown for a moment into a temporary state of embarrassment. The poor animal, however, unconscious that it had transgressed any forbidden limit, went on quite smoothly with the remainder of the piece, which passed off in excellent style.

The Intelligence, **Sunday 20 June 1830**
(v.85, p.138)

~

IMPORTANT DECISION

A gentleman, who had been described as a 'Pettifogger,' accused another gentleman, whom he had styled a 'Fish-fag,' with an assault. It being a very intricate point, it was of course referred to the Lord Mayor. It stood as follows: – 'Whether puffing a cloud of tobacco-smoke in a man's face constituted an assault?' After some grave consultation with that encyclopaedia of wisdom, Mr. Hobler, the decision ran thus – The Lord Mayor: 'There has been no assault; nothing but words, words.' – Complainant: 'I beg pardon, my Lord.' – The Lord Mayor: 'Well, then, all smoke, if you please, or words and *puffs*. There have been no *blows*.' – Now we beg his Lordship's pardon. Pray what is a *puff* but a *blow*?

***The Age*, Sunday 8 August 1830 (v.85, p.203)**

~

WONDERFUL WONDERS

The chin-chopping gentleman who is now
exhibiting will, we understand, be soon rivalled by
a lady, who plays the key-bugle with her toes, blows
the pandean pipes with her nose, and plays the
castanets with her teeth.

The Age, Sunday 8 August 1830 (v.85, p.203)

At the Durham Assizes, on Monday, an action was brought by a farmer named Hart, against another farmer, named Young, and some of his family, to recover damages for assault. The parties had been upon bad terms for some years, in consequence of a dispute concerning the boundaries of their respective farms. Upon the evening of the 6th July last, the plaintiff sent out two of his workmen to make some alterations in the hedges which parted the farms, and these men were at their work when the elder defendant came and interrupted them. High words ensued, and the plaintiff joined his men, which junction of forces was deemed sufficient to bring against him the whole array of the defendant's family; the latter, joined by two of his daughters, came down, vi et armis, with pitchforks, flails, and other weapons of the homestead and barn-yard, and a fray ensued in which some of the women were severely handled. Blood was visible on the field, and fragments of combs, locks of hair, torn caps, and laces, adorned the trophies of the combatants. Some of these were exhibited in the court, and a cudgel was also brought forth in evidence of the Amazonian prowess of the damsels engaged. The plaintiff was confined to his bed in consequence of the injuries he received. – Verdict for the plaintiff, Damages, Fifty Pounds.

Bell's Life in London, Sunday 15 August 1830
(v.85, p.216)

~

A REALLY ROTTEN BOROUGH

At the election at Lymington, if election it may be called, since a seat there is a marketable commodity, a very unpleasant accident occurred to one of the candidates, but whether it happened to this gentleman or to that gentleman our delicacy forbids us to mention. Whether this action was produced by the great exertion of speaking, whether owing to an overwhelming sense of the duties devolving on him, or whether brought about by some secret operations, cannot be ascertained; but if the *cause* was involved in obscurity, the effect soon became too evident to be denied. By the kindness of a special reporter we are able to lay before our readers what the honourable candidate said on this interesting occasion: – 'Gentlemen, I am really taken by surprise at this present moment, not having made the necessary arrangements prior to coming to the hustings. I have very little to say about my future operations in parliament, but I hope that I shall never make a motion which will leave me in bad odour with my constituents. When I take my seat in the House, or if I should become a Privy Councillor, I will do all I can to purge the body politic so as to restore the pristine vigour of the constitution.'

The Age, Sunday 15 August 1830 (v.85, p.219)

~

OBITUARIES

The Waterford Chronicle requests that persons supplying the Journal with obituaries will attend to the following scale of prices (the idea is droll); for a simple death two shillings and sixpence. For the death of a person deeply regretted, five shillings. For the death of a person who lived a perfect pattern of all the Christian virtues, and died regretted by the whole country, ten shillings. For the death of a person who possessed extensive literature and profound erudition, superadded to which, his whole life was remarkable for piety, humility, charity, and self-denial, one pound. For the death of a lady, whose husband is inconsolable for her loss, and who was the delight of the circle in which she moved, one pound ten shillings. For the death of a gentleman, who had only been six months married, who was an example of every conjugal and domestic virtue, and whose widow is in a state of anguish bordering on distraction, two pounds. For the death of an aristocrat, who was a pattern of meekness, a model of humility, a patron of distressed genius, a genuine philanthropist, an exemplary Christian, an extensive alms-giver, profoundly learned, unremitting to the duties of his station, kind, hospitable, and affectionate to his tenantry, and whose name will be remembered and his loss deplored to the latest posterity, five pounds. For every additional good quality, whether domestic, moral, or religious, there will be an additional charge.

Birmingham Journal, **Saturday 21 August 1830**
(v.85, p.225)

~

THE DEAD ALIVE

The papers – there really is no believing one single word they say – have all conspired to put an end to the mortal and political career of that staunch and uncompromising patriot, Sir Compton Domville, Bart. The press of England, Ireland, and Scotland had, in the most pathetic and touching terms – 'deeply regretted' – 'sincerely lamented' – and 'unfeignedly deplored the sad event that deprived his family of an exemplary husband, father, and friend, the State of a most efficient senator, and society of one of its most valuable members' when, lo and behold! there suddenly appears a short *par*, like the postscript of a lady's letter, containing the most agreeable and important intelligence of all: – 'We are happy to be able, upon the very best authority (viz. of the Baronet himself), to contradict the report so generally and circumstantially circulated, of the death of Sir C. Domville; he is alive and in perfect health.' Your every-day newspaper people are *incorrigible* romancers.

The Age, Sunday 24 July 1831 (v.86, p.127)

~

DRAM-DRINKING

At a late meeting in Manchester the practice of dram-drinking was reprobated in very strong terms, and among other proofs of its bad consequences, it was stated that according to authentic records, about twenty deaths were caused by it annually in the town alone. Two dram shops in Manchester, it was mentioned, sold £120 worth of ardent spirits on one day; another took on the average £150 per day; and at another on one day in June last, customers had entered at the rate of 500 an hour, of which number six-tenths were women, three-tenths respectable looking females, and one-tenth girls! Without intending a pun, it may be said that such exhibitions of public spirit should, if possible, be prevented; and so thought those who attended the meeting, as they adopted resolutions of temperance and sobriety in future.

Birmingham Journal, Sunday 1 January 1831
(v.86, p.192)

~

BISCUIT MACHINE

The Navy Board is manufacturing biscuits at Portsmouth by machinery. The first process is that of mixing the meal (5 cwt.) with a sufficient quantity of water, which is accomplished in two minutes; the second process is that of rolling the dough, which is placed on boards, to its proper thickness; and the third and last process is passing the dough, when rolled, under the stamping machines, which will stamp the extraordinary number of 360 per minute, or 21,600 per hour. The whole of these operations are performed without the dough coming into contact with the hand or any other part of the body, and the machines perform their respective duties with admirable precision, expedition, and cleanliness, and have answered the most sanguine expectations of their spirited inventor.

***The Age*, Sunday 5 September 1830 (v.85, p.277)**

~

TAXATION

A tax upon industry is most impolitic, for it must check the national energies. There are times, however, when that which is good in principle may be bad in application. An evening paper asserts, 'that Government intends to lay a tax upon steam power; that is, we presume, upon locomotive power, and the engines of steam vessels – very fair objects of taxation under existing circumstances.' We ascribe much of the present distress, not to the use of improved machinery, but to the suddenness of introduction. All sudden changes must be followed by temporary distress; but when men throw off the prejudice of the old habits, and see the advantages to be derived from change, the spirit of discontent, and with it the real grievance, is removed. This new tax cannot be deemed impolitic at the present time: the interests of the hard working have suffered, and they of all classes ought to be protected.

The Age, Sunday 19 December 1830
(v.86, p.151)

∼

WILTSHIRE COMMISSION

This commission was opened at Salisbury on Friday week, and the trials of the prisoners commenced on Saturday. There were upwards of 300 prisoners for trial; of these nearly 9 out of 12 were charged with the destruction of machinery. In most of the cases of robbery and destruction of machinery they were charged with having been done riotously and tumultuously. There were several charged with pulling down a house; one with setting fire to a threshing machine. From the serious nature of some of the charges it is not likely that the business of the commission will end for a week, if so soon.

***Bell's Life in London*, Sunday 9 January 1831 (v.86, p.220)**

NEWS RAISONNEE

MACHINERY

We read 'Such is the indiscriminate rage against machinery, that a sausage-maker in Portsmouth has been compelled to lay aside his pork-chopper for the present.' The dentists expect being visited very shortly on account of their grinding machines.

***The Age*, Sunday 26 December 1830 (v.86, p.165)**

❖

We understand that the cotton net made by machinery, which was sold some years ago at 4*s*. 6*d*. per yard, can now be bought at 2*d*. Such is the case with articles made in the neighbourhood of Exeter, and such the difference of price in the short space of less than 20 years, through the improvement of machinery used for this manufacture.

Bell's Life in London, **Sunday 9 January 1831**

(v.86, p.219)

His Majesty was solicited the other day to patronise the Russian Horn Players, who had the honour of performing at the Royal Palace, when his Majesty replied, that 'these were not the times to bestow his patronage upon every novelty of foreign birth.' His Majesty, in this instance, has shown his wisdom.

Bell's Life in London, **Sunday 2 January 1831**
(v.86, p.195)

~

THE DRAMA:

CHRISTMAS PANTOMIMES

Drury Lane Theatre

At this house, after the tragedy of *Jane Shore*, the impatient 'Gods' were delighted by the commencement of the pantomime, under the title *Davy Jones, or Harlequin and Mother Carey's Chickens*. The opening scenes, in which the mischievous tricks of Mother Carey and her brood are portrayed, contain a laughable burlesque on the nautical drama of *Black-ey'd Susan*, which is ridiculed in a pleasant and good-humoured manner.

Covent Garden Theatre

The Grecian Daughter, with the attraction of Miss. Fanny Kemble, kept the boisterous part of the audience in tolerable order till the pantomime commenced, and then all eyes and ears were fixed in delighted attention. The title of this piece is *Harlequin Pat and Harlequin Bat, or The Giant's Causeway*. The introduction, instead of consisting of a ballet action, had a speaking opening, and was graced by the comic drollery of Mr. Power, who appeared for the first time, much to his own surprise, in the character of a harlequin. The author of the introduction has ventured on the experiment rather more bold than fortunate, of exhibiting an embodied echo, for Rhadamisthus O'Mullingar (Mr. Power) drags it forward from its hiding place and threatens it with punishment for not replying to his questions as an Irish echo is bound to do, instead of repeating them.

The Adelphi Theatre

The pantomime at this house is called *Grimalkin the Great, or Harlequin King of the Cats*; and, considering the limited size of the house, went off with great e-*claw*, and embraced several good hits at passing events. The scene opens with a view of a great mouse-trap maker's house, with a conspiracy of the cats to destroy his traps or machinery because they put them out of employ.

Bell's Life in London, **Sunday 2 January 1831** **(v.86, p.195)**

~

HOW TO CATCH A THIEF

At Bow-street on Wednesday, a decent-looking man of the name of William Marks, was placed at the bar, on a charge made against him by Mr. Spenser, a spirit- and wine-merchant, residing in Newton-street, Holborn. It appeared from the statement of the prosecutor, that he had lately missed a great quantity of valuable wine from his cellar, amongst which was some old Malmsey Madeira, which he valued at twenty guineas a dozen. He had not, although he had exercised a great deal of caution, been able to discover the thief, nor should he, had his son not informed him of a most likely expedient wherewith to obtain the desired information. This was to put a detonating ball in the keyhole of the cellar, and sure enough it proved the means of discovering the thief. The proceeding night they were startled by a loud explosion, and on going down stairs, they found the prisoner standing before the door, seemingly petrified, and unable to account for what had taken place. A false key was in his hand, and at once explained the way in which he had so long escaped detection. He confessed that he was the thief, and that he himself had drunk all the wine which had been missed. The prisoner, who is a servant at the house next door to that of the prosecutor, said nothing in his defence, and was remanded, to give time for the production of further evidence.

Bell's Life in London, **Sunday 16 January 1831**
(v.86, p.230)

~

THE MONUMENT

The chipping off the old inscription has begun. This is abundantly silly. To mutilate and destroy inscriptions is to falsify history. Its remaining there did not prove that the Catholics set fire to the city, but it proved the bigoted ignorance of the people who believed so; it proved that popular opinions, where they run current with popular prejudice, are very indifferent authority.

The Age, **Sunday 30 January 1831 (v.86, p.273)**

~

THE PATHETIC

A 'Contemporary Journal' puts forth the following piece of condolence: – 'We regret to announce the decease of Her Royal Highness, Louisa Landgravine of Schleswig Holstein, which took place at Schleswig, between eleven and twelve o'clock, during the night of the 12th ult.' – If we could pronounce the word Schleswig with due emphasis and discretion, we would ejaculate our grief also. The expressions of regret which flow from the sympathising bosoms of numerous journalists, become frequently, what they ought not, a subject of mirth. The ministerial paper of last week said – 'We deeply regret to state that Lord Holland has had another slight attack of the gout.' Now really this is not a very mournful business.

The Age, Sunday 6 February 1831 (v.86, p.289)

~

ADVANTAGES OF

DOWNING STREET

As this street has been the scene of so much political business, it may be worth knowing what are its peculiar advantages. Lord North spoke of it as follows: – 'The street is narrow at its entrance, and consequently can be easily defended, and it has no other outlet. The house, though large behind, yet presents but a small front, having there only three windows on a floor; and in case of necessity, there is an easy access behind, for receiving military aid from the Horse Guards, where troops are always stationed.' Prime Ministers, now-a-days, are compelled to give way to public opinion, however they may affect to despise it. This is far more powerful than a thousand brigades.

The Age, **Sunday 6 February 1831 (v.86, p.289)**

David Fairs, a pauper in Romford workhouse, was indicted for stealing a purse, containing eight shillings, from another pauper, named Joseph Dill. The prisoner was found Guilty. – The learned Judge remarked that it was quite clear the prisoner was unfit to remain in the country and therefore sentenced him to be transported for fourteen years. – The prosecutor excited considerable laughter in the court by the ludicrous manner in which he gave his evidence, particularly one answer to a question by the learned Judge. 'Were you in liquor at the time of the robbery?' Witness: 'Oh, no! I was as sober as a Judge.' The learned Baron joined heartily in the universal laugh.

Bell's Life in London, **Sunday 13 March 1831 (v.87, p.33)**

~

IMPRUDENCE OF A SMILE

A very singular occurrence took place a few days ago at Newtown, near Bannow, in this county. A clergyman was in the act of tying the nuptial knot between a young couple in the above parish, and had proceeded in the ceremony as far as the words 'wedded wife' when the risible faculties of the embryo bridegroom manifested themselves in a broad grin. The officiating clergyman, not deeming such levity consistent with the rites of so solemn a ceremony, desisted from finishing the holy rite, and left the laughing swain with only *half* the claims of a husband. However, at the entreaties of some friends, and a promise on the part of the bridegroom to be more serious for the future, he was, at a late hour the same evening, in the village of Carrick, made a *full* spouse, by having the ceremony completed.

The Morning Herald, **Monday 14 March 1831**
(v.87, p.47)

CURIOUS INVENTION

An ingenious mechanic, in the neighbourhood of Hull, has invented a small lamp, which may be attached to spectacles of a particular description, by means of which and a reflector any person may read in the darkest night, and the contrivance is such, that the only light visible is on the part of the book that is read.

Conception-Bay Mercury, Friday 16 July 1830 (v.87, p.102)

A selection from The Prophetic Messenger _for 1832:_

GOOD AND EVIL DAYS

JAN – … we may expect fires, accidents, shipwrecks, or noted calamities …

4   Wednesday a good day for all matters wherein writings or papers are concerned

FEB – … one of the cleverest dies, perhaps mathematician, or one noted for public skill …

1   Wednesday is quarrelsome & evil.

4   Saturday is truly evil in all things.

17   Friday, evil-dangerous, shun all adventures.

MAR – … the fires of heaven burn brightly; but it is to *warn* us mortals, they are hung out as tokens of impending evil …

15   Thursday is one of the most evil of all the days.

APR – … A Military general or great commander dies! Plots assail one of the rich …

11   Wednesday. Do not travel or marry.

26   Thursday is one of the best days in the month for marriage, journeys or adventures.

MAY – … Far be it from me to terrify mankind by my predictions of evil – the seeds of a vast and singular crisis, perchance of a new era in the political hemisphere, are sown.

5   Saturday is a good day for all expeditious matters

JUN – … statesmen, mercurialists, and public writers are amenable to trouble, the clergy are unfortunate …

20   Wednesday. The after-part of this day is singularly propitious.

JUL – … Mighty events will soon happen in Turkey and the Oriental states, where the slow but fatal march of Saturn will work divers wonders …

1   Sunday. Until the afternoon, nothing can be more unfortunate.

AUG – ... The Grim King of Terrors is ſtretching forth his gigantic arms; he ſtrikes down one of the greateſt. Many suicides and ſtrange deaths will happen.

13   Monday. Be careful this day. Naught will proſper.

26   Saturday is another evil day in all cogitations, but is ſtill worse in all money matters.

SEPT – ... Secret conſpiracies are afloat; and a chapter of unusual accidents and disaſters swell out of the record of the month ...

25   Wednesday. Woo, marry, travel, &c.

OCT – ... A disaſtrous shipwreck is among the ſtarry presages; and much sudden, ſtrange, and extraordinary news will soon arrive from abroad ...

25   Thursday. Marry, sell or buy.

NOV – ... At home a royal or dignified person is vilified or afflicted ...

9   Friday is a hazardous day.

17   Saturday is unproſperous, evil, and mischievous.

DEC – ... Thousands will be hurried to the gloomy vaults of death ... The year concluded highly unfortunate for both rich and poor ...

21   Friday, evil.

Printed by J. Viar, 48, Holywell-ſtreet, Strand.

(v.88, p.214)

~

HOUSE OF COMMONS

Wednesday, March 28

Cholera

Mr. G Dawson adverted to the opposition that was made by some poor Irish families to the removal of the dead bodies of their friends who had died of cholera, until they had remained the usual time. At present the parish authorities had not sufficient power to enforce the removal, which should take place as early as possible. Mr. G. Lamb said that he would admit that in such cases Government ought to interfere.

The Observer, **Sunday 1 April 1832 (v.90, p.6)**

~

CHOLERAPHOBIA

A woman named Sanderland, the wife of an Irish Schoolmaster, residing at 20, George-street, Grosvenor-square, was suddenly taken ill while walking in the park with her husband. She immediately returned home, where she was seized with violent retchings, accompanied by relaxations in the bowels. Mr. Symes, the parish surgeon, was sent for, who rendered her assistance, but ultimately sent for Mr. Ainsworth, as he deemed it a case of cholera; and that gentleman attended her until her death, which took place on Monday morning, at ten o'clock. The deceased was in an advanced state of pregnancy, and it was the opinion of her husband that she had died in labour, and not of cholera. On the part of the medical gentlemen it was positively asserted to be a case of cholera, and reported accordingly. Some resistance being expected in the removal of the body for interment in the place appropriated for cholera patients, eight or nine, accompanied by a body of police, repaired to the house in George-ſtreet. On arrival there they found their fears verified, and the room filled with countrymen of the deceased who, in no measured terms, defied them to touch the corpse until an inqueſt was held to inquire into the circumſtances attending the death of the woman. The surgeons, who had attended the deceased, gave their opinions that she died of cholera. The Jury returned a verdiċt that 'the deceased died by the visitation of God.' Some disapproval was expressed at the verdiċt by the crowd outside, and several of the medical gentlemen were hissed.

Bell's Life in London, Sunday 1 April 1832 (v.90, p.26)

~

ANOTHER CHOLERA

DISTURBANCE

For several hours on Friday afternoon the neighbourhood of Earl-street East, Lisson-grove, was a scene of complete uproar, owing to the following circumstance: Between one and two o'clock a young man, of the name of Young, an assistant to Mr. Holton, surgeon, &c., of Lisson-grove, accompanied by a party of men with an accommodation chair, proceeded to the house, No. 40, in Earl-street, for the purpose of conveying an elderly man, named Bengal, a shoe-maker, who had been labouring under cholera, to Marylebone Cholera Hospital, at Camden Town. It appears that the patient was willing to be taken thither, and the Doctor and his party sallied forth into the street with their patient stretched out in the accommodation chair, which was similar in shape to a child's crib. At this period a mob of upwards of 600 people (chiefly Irish) assembled. They followed the Doctor's party pretty orderly along Earl-street and Salisbury-street till they arrived at Church-street, where the mob was greatly increased, and a hue and cry was raised 'that they were going to Burke the man.' The chair was instantly seized, and the poor fellow, in a state of nudity, was pulled out, some tugging on one side, and some on another. At length he was placed in a lifeless state on a man's back, and conveyed, amidst an immense multitude, to his residence, the Doctor and his party following with an empty chair. On their arriving in Earl-street, the mob commenced a furious attack on the Doctor and his party – the chair was torn to atoms, and they were pelted with its fragments. A policeman was knocked down by a stomach-warmer, and the surgeon sought refuge (after getting a black eye) in a chandler's shop.

The patient, notwithstanding his treatment, is expected to recover.

Bell's Life in London, Sunday 1 April 1832
(v.90, p.26)

~

THE CHOLERA REPORT

We mention with deep regret the intelligence communicated to us yesterday by very respectable authority that the country people, between Tullamore and Ballinasloe, assembled in great numbers on Monday night last, and proceeded to cut down the banks of the Grand Canal, running to the latter town. They accomplished this object in five or six places in such a manner as to interrupt all communication by the Canal. We understand they were impelled to this rash and indefensible act of outrage by the impression now very prevalent among them, that it was owing to the communication by water that cholera was carried throughout the interior of the country with such rapidity; and, of course, they hoped to prevent further and continued dissemination of the fatal malady among them by this means.

[NOTE: One of the features of cholera that inspired such fear was the not knowing how the infection was passed on. Like many, Dr Jahinicren of Moscow firmly believed that: 'the disease is neither directly, or indirectly, contagious or epidemic, but that it derives its origin from some specific miasma, or areal poison in the atmosphere: at the same time that the predisposing cause, whether arising from a gaseous miasma, poisonous vapour from vegetable putrefaction, or any other original source, would be greatly aided by a person in health being compelled to breathe the air of a house or hospital where the disease already exists.' (*The Morning Post*, Thursday 9 June 1831)]

(From *The Dublin Morning Register*)

The Englishman (town edition), Sunday 24 June 1832 (v.91, p.52)

~

THE BRITISH MUSEUM

'The characteristic of the British populace – perhaps we ought to say people, for it extends to the middle classes – is their propensity to mischief. The people of most other countries may be safely admitted into parks, gardens, public buildings, and galleries of pictures, and statues; but in England it is necessary to exclude them, as much as possible, from all such places.'

This is a sentence from the last published number of the 'Quarterly Review.' Severe as it is, there is much truth in it. We hope to do something, speaking generally, to excite and gratify a taste for intellectual pleasure; but we wish to do more in this particular case. We wish to point out many inexpensive pleasures, of the very highest order, which all those who reside in London have within their reach.

Well, then, that we may waste no time in general discussion, let us begin with the BRITISH MUSEUM. We will suppose ourselves addressing an artisan or tradesman, who can sometimes afford to take a holiday, and who knows there are better modes of spending a working day, which he some half-dozen times a year devotes to pleasure, than amidst the smoke of a tap-room or the din of a skittle-ground. Well, then, in Great Russell-street, Bloomsbury, is the British Museum; and here, from ten o'clock till four, on Mondays, Wednesdays, and Fridays, he may see many of the choicest productions of ancient art. 'But hold,' says the working man, 'I have passed by the British Museum: there are two sentinels at the gate way, and the large gates are always closed. Will they let me in? Is there nothing to pay?' *Here* there *is* nothing to pay. Knock boldly at the gate; the porter will open it. Go on. Do not fear any surly looks or impertinent glances from any person in attendance. You are upon safe ground here. You are come to see your own property. You have as much right to see it as the highest in the land. Your garb is homely, you think, as you see gaily dressed persons going in and out. No matter; you, your wife, and your children are clean, if not smart. It will be necessary to observe a few simple rules.

1st. *Touch nothing.* The statues and other curious things, which are in the Museum, are to be seen, not handled. If visitors were to be allowed to touch them, to try whether they were hard or soft, to scratch them, to write upon them with their pencils, they would soon be worth very little.

2ndly. *Do not talk loud.* Do not call loudly from one end of a long gallery to the other, or you will distract the attention of those who derive great enjoyment from an undisturbed contemplation of the wonders of these rooms.

3rdly. *Be not obtrusive.* You will see many things in the Museum that you do not understand. It will be well to make a memorandum of these, to be inquired into at your leisure. But do not trouble other visitors with your questions, and above all do not trouble the young artists, some of whom you will see making drawings for their improvement. You must not expect to understand what you see, you must go again and again if you wish to obtain real knowledge, beyond the gratification of passing curiosity.

The Penny Magazine of the Society for the Diffusion of Useful Knowledge,
Saturday 7 April 1832 (v.90, p.33)

~

AN ADDRESS TO PERSONS

WHO ENTERTAIN THE WISH

TO BETTER THEMSELVES BY

EMIGRATING TO CANADA

London, 1832.

We have read with a good deal of interest a small and cheap pamphlet entitled 'An address to persons who entertain the wish to better themselves by Emigrating to Canada, as well as to parish officers, churchwardens, and overseers, and all concerned in providing for the poor of Great Britain.' It contains much valuable information, and a great deal of good advice. The following is an extract –

First, we shall candidly pronounce who ought NOT to go there, in order that all such persons may save themselves from certain disappointment, after they shall have undergone the fatigue and expense of a long voyage: – viz.

Those who are happily situated at home, maintaining their families comfortably, and who are able to lay by sufficient for their support in old age, and for the eligible establishment of their children.

Those who have nothing but birth or wealth to recommend them, or who have no useful occupation. – In Canada, as in England, it is the active working bee, and not the drone, that gathers the honey to the hive.

Those who are of a restless, factious, and quarrelsome frame of mind, or those who think that in Canada every one, however wrong-headed, can do whatever is right in his own eyes, without regard to either law, justice, or decorum. Canada is a land of liberty, but it also has its laws, to which all persons, without distinction, must submit.

Those who expect to make a fortune suddenly, without much exertion – those who are indolent, or of dissolute habits – ardent spirits being excessively cheap, all those who cannot refrain from a too-free use of them are certain to bring on, rapidly, premature disease, disgrace, and death.

Those who are not seriously disposed to industry and economy had better stay away.

The importance of this subject may be estimated from the fact of upwards of 50,000 emigrants having left this country for the Canadas laſt year, and from the probability that double this number will leave during the present.

Birmingham Journal, **Saturday 1 April 1832**
(v.90, p.31)

We could name ten individuals, within the circle of half-a-mile from Fenchurch-ſtreet, who possess ten millions of property, and who do not altogether contribute as much to the State, in taxes, as any ten shopkeepers in any town in the kingdom. Is not this faƈt sufficient to rouse the honeſt indignation of every tradesman who labours incessantly to pay taxes, and to uphold and support his family, who, after all his toil and anxiety, is but too often the viƈtim of this cruel, inequitable syſtem of taxation?

Birmingham Journal, **Saturday 28 April 1832**
(v.90, p.70)

~

COMMERCIAL REMARKS:

CHINA

Cotton

Still little spirit seems to exist in the market, and many of the recent cargoes remain in the hands of the consignees, waiting for better prices.

Pearls

Pearls still find a very unfavourable return in the market. There are no Mother o Pearl shells in the place.

Nakin raw silk

Several parcels have been received, and a few of the early arrivals have been sold; but the intelligence of the rapid fall in the price of this article in England, and of the deplorable situation of the manufactures in that country, has checked all speculation.

Opium

In opium some few bargains have been made in the last week or two – but principal sales have been in small lots for cash, and prices have been daily declining. It is reported by the people arriving from the interior that the Mandarins have been very troublesome in several of the provinces, and have much interfered with the retailers of the drug, which discourages the dealers here from offering high prices, and entering into any considerable contracts. The last sales, we understand, were made at $670 per Pecul, but $700 is the price now talked of.

The Canton Register, **Monday 17 August 1829**
(v.90, p.74)

~

INVERTING TREES

In the course of ascertaining how far a circulation of sap is carried on in trees, some interesting facts have been determined by Mr. Knight and others with regard to the effects of inverted stems, or in other words of planting the superior part of the stem, and thus converting it into a root. If the stem of a plum or cherry tree, which, if not too thick, be bent, and the top be put under ground, while the roots are gradually detached, in proportion as the former top of the stem becomes firmly fixed in the soil the branches of the root will shoot forth leaves and flower, and in due time will produce fruit.

Birmingham Journal, Saturday 19 May 1832 (v.90, p.138)

~

REFORM ACT

We consider no public subject of so much moment and immediate importance as a right understanding of the privileges and duties of Constituents, and the claims of Candidates to public confidence. Under the corrupt system of the expiring nomination and rotten borough – falsely called representation – the relative obligations of Voter and Representative were little thought of and still less respected. The ordinary and most influential qualifications of a Member of Parliament were aristocratic rank, or *blood*; money and its profligate expenditure in bribes and treating; means of obtaining and dispensing Government patronage, and the personal qualities of 'a good electioneer.' But a new era has commenced, and it is the most sacred duty of a Journalist to submit the pretentions of every local candidate to the test of the national interest. The first reformed parliament will be an experimental assembly. It will take some time for the old Borough and Country constituency to get rid of prejudices and corruptions, and for the voters of newly enfranchised towns to understand and exercise their electoral rights. The common observation every where is the paucity of candidates duly qualified, and the fallacy of claims put forward in the public addresses of those who are seeking the responsible office of *Representatives*.

Birmingham Journal, **Saturday 16 June 1832**
(v.91, p.1)

~

ASPLEY HOUSE

His Grace the Duke of Wellington is busily engaged in providing himself with ample protection against the celebration of the reform bill – on which occasion his Grace seems to expect a display of the estimation of his conduct. From morn till night, the 'note of preparation,' and 'the clank of hammers closing rivets up,' may be heard through the mansion; to the windows of which, even including the attics, iron shutters are being affixed, of a strength and substance sufficient to resist a musket ball – several trials to that effect having been made on Tuesday last, with a rifle piece, from the garden in the park.

Birmingham Journal, **Saturday 16 June 1832**
(v.91, p.5)

~

THE LOVE OF SONG

A young man, an apprentice to a cheesemonger, in Whitechapel, acting under the influence of a desire to excel himself in singing, last week performed an operation on himself, which, according to his own belief, is likely to place him on a par with the celebrated Veluti. He effected his purpose so skilfully, that, on going to Mr. Andrews, the surgeon of the London Hospital, that gentleman applied the proper dressings, and the lad is doing well. He said he had

been studying books on surgery to qualify himself
for the task.

Bell's Life in London, **Sunday 17 June 1832 (v.91, p.9)**

~

THE POT-BOY BEFORE

THE BIG WIGS

In the court of King's Bench, on Monday, a young
man of the name of Black, a pot-boy in Dickinson's
public-house and tavern, Regent's-park, appeared
to receive the sentence of the Court for a violation
and contempt of its authority under the following
circumstances: – His master apprehended an arrest,
and kept aloof of the Sheriff's officers, who made
several ineffectual attempts to execute their warrant,
which was issued by the Court. On one occasion
they came to the house and demanded admittance
to a particular apartment, which was closed.
A young woman from the inside declared that
Dickinson was not there, and alleged as a reason for
her refusal to open the door, that she was undressed,

and preparing to dress. However, the gallantry of the bailiffs was not of that chivalrous and disinterested stamp as to induce them to value female delicacy before parchment, and they proceeded to break open the door. The pot-boy rushed forward, and gave them some *striking* evidence of what he thought of their conduct. A fight ensued, and for some time the proceedings were directed by might rather than right. They wrestled, kicked, struck, and bit. It was a regular *pancration* fight. The bailiffs were severely handled, and the pot-boy got a bite that disabled him from earning his bread for three months.

Bell's Life in London, **Sunday 17 June 1832**
(v.91, p.16)

❖

The remains of Mr. Jeremy Bentham were anatomized, according to his last request, at the Medical theatre of Mr. Grainger, in Webb-street, Borough, on Monday last. The lecturer took some occasion to point out the immense advantage that had been derived by mankind by the pursuit of this most important study.

Bell's Life in London, **Sunday 17 June 1832**
(v.91, p.15)

~

DIVING

There is a small cutter now lying in Yarmouth belonging to a man named Bell. Her crew consists of six men, several of whom are singularly expert in diving. She sails about from place to place to offer assistance to recover lost treasure, &c. She has arrived for the purpose (by permission of the Admiralty) of endeavouring to obtain a portion of the treasure lost in the *Guernsey Lily* transport, which got on the Cross Sand, floated off, and afterwards foundered in the centre of the Yarmouth-roads, in 43 feet of water, coming with stores from Holland, after the Duke of York's expedition in 1799. The transport was laden with horses, ammunition (in which were 25 brass field pieces), a stock of wine, &c. The method these divers use is curious: – The cutter is first placed immediately over the wreck; the diver, then, habited in an India-rubber air-tight dress, having a tube attached at the back of the neck to receive the air (which is constantly kept pumping in), descends from a rope ladder, and gives signals for certain things to be sent down by a small line, which is attended to by those on the deck of the cutter; by this line baskets and other utensils are sent down for the use of the diver, and sent up again with wine, &c., taken from the wreck. The diver's head-dress is curious; it is composed of copper, and is a complete covering, made much after the manner of an ancient helmet, only that it is much larger than the head, and has in its upper part three glass windows; it weighs 50lb. He carries down with him 120lb. of lead in two bags. With all this weight he declares that when in the water he appears perfectly free from weight or encumbrance of any sort. There has already been brought up a large quantity of wine (the bottles curiously tattooed with large and small oysters, which have been tasted, and are excellent), some copper, iron handles of chests, and gun-carriages, &c. They hope soon to be in possession of the brass guns, valuable plate, and the dollars which it was known the transport had on board for the purpose of paying the troops employed in the above mentioned expedition.

The Morning Post, **Wednesday 15 August 1832 (v.91, p.220)**

~

BITING OFF A MAN'S NOSE

At Hatton-garden, on Wednesday last, a miscreant named Patrick O'Keefe was charged with the following horrible assault on James McCarthy: – The complainant's wife having quarrelled with the prisoner's sister at a public house near Gray's Inn-lane, the prisoner struck McCarthy, and a struggle ensued, when O'Keefe seized the complainant's nose between his teeth and bit it clean off. McCarthy said he had taken great pains to find the part bitten off, under an impression that he could have it stuck on, but without effect, and O'Keefe boasted of having swallowed it. The complainant, whose face was covered in plaster, seemed much depressed in consequence of his misfortune. The prisoner was fined five pounds, and in default of payment committed.

Bell's Life in London, **Sunday 19 August 1832**
(v.91, p.244)

~

ERRATA

TO THE EDITOR OF THE TIMES
Sir,

Having seen in a Sunday paper a receipt for making a pleasant cooling beverage, in which the reader is directed to mix carbonate of soda with nitric acid, I think it cannot be too soon made known to the public that nitric acid is a violent poison. It is, no doubt, a misprint for citric acid, as 'acid of lemon' immediately follows in a parenthesis; but as many individuals may send to their chymists for nitric acid, without accompanying it with an explanation, it is to be feared that some lives may be lost by this oversight. The editor of the Sunday paper alluded to will of course correct it in his next publication. This cannot, however, be done before a week has elapsed. I therefore entreat that you will, in the mean time, do all in your power, by means of your journal, to prevent the fatal effects which may arise from this mistake. I am, Sir, your obedient servant.
HUMANITAS

The Times, Tuesday 30 August 1825 (v.71, p.261)

~

A LONG RUN

A provincial paper states that a new light coach is to run from *June* to *Weymouth*.

The Age, Sunday 13 June 1830 (v.85, p.79)

~

CONNUBIAL CERBERUS

The following announcement of a marriage is somewhat singular. It would seem that Baron Roebeck, having found one wife at a time too much for him, has now ventured on three at once: –

'Married, at Paris, at the British Ambassador's Chapel, the Baron de Robeck, to Emily Elizabeth, eldest daughter of John Josþeh Henry, Esq., of the county of Tipperary, and the Right Hon. Lady Emily Henry, and niece of his Grace the Duke of Leinster'!!!

Three notes of admiration can scarcely express our wonder at this act of *trigamy!*

The Age, Sunday 24 July 1831 (v.86, p.127)

There was an error in a note to the report of the Lords' Committee upon privilege in our paper of yesterday. Mr. James Redmond Barry, who now claims the Viscountcy of the late Barrymore peerage, is a gentleman from the county of Cork, and unconnected with the unfortunate person who was the subject of a coroner's inquest on Wednesday, with whom he was confounded in the note.

The Times, Saturday 18 June 1825 (v.70, p.61)

**Visit our website and discover thousands
of other History Press books.**

www.thehistorypress.co.uk